Louise Brigham and the Early History of Sustainable Furniture Design

Antoinette LaFarge

Louise Brigham and the Early History of Sustainable Furniture Design

palgrave
macmillan

Antoinette LaFarge
University of California, Irvine
Irvine, CA, USA

ISBN 978-3-030-32340-0   ISBN 978-3-030-32341-7 (eBook)
https://doi.org/10.1007/978-3-030-32341-7

© The Editor(s) (if applicable) and The Author(s), under exclusive license to Springer Nature Switzerland AG 2019
This work is subject to copyright. All rights are solely and exclusively licensed by the Publisher, whether the whole or part of the material is concerned, specifically the rights of translation, reprinting, reuse of illustrations, recitation, broadcasting, reproduction on microfilms or in any other physical way, and transmission or information storage and retrieval, electronic adaptation, computer software, or by similar or dissimilar methodology now known or hereafter developed.
The use of general descriptive names, registered names, trademarks, service marks, etc. in this publication does not imply, even in the absence of a specific statement, that such names are exempt from the relevant protective laws and regulations and therefore free for general use.
The publisher, the authors and the editors are safe to assume that the advice and information in this book are believed to be true and accurate at the date of publication. Neither the publisher nor the authors or the editors give a warranty, expressed or implied, with respect to the material contained herein or for any errors or omissions that may have been made. The publisher remains neutral with regard to jurisdictional claims in published maps and institutional affiliations.

Cover illustration: © John Rawsterne/patternhead.com, Edgar Cayce Readings © 1971, 1993–2007 The Edgar Cayce Foundation. All Rights Reserved.

This Palgrave Pivot imprint is published by the registered company Springer Nature Switzerland AG
The registered company address is: Gewerbestrasse 11, 6330 Cham, Switzerland

*Dedicated to my mother:
Maria Barbera Boissevain La Farge,
the first feminist in my life*

Preface

This book owes its existence to my penchant for rummaging in archives. One day, hunting about among documents at the Institute of Cultural Inquiry in Los Angeles, I discovered a tattered copy of the *Ladies' Home Journal* from 1910. Leafing through it, I came across an illustration of Louise Brigham's dining room, accompanying one of her several articles for the *LHJ* on the subject of furniture made from recycled boxes. This image fairly leaped off the page at me, the starkness of Brigham's rectilinear box furniture startling in its contrast with the plush and cozy home furnishings illustrated throughout the rest of the issue. Intrigued, I started to tug on this thread that chance had dropped in my lap: who was this Louise Brigham, and why hadn't I heard of her? One thing led to another, and before too long I was writing what I initially thought would be a fairly straightforward essay about her work with box furniture. As I delved into her life, however, I found a wide array of links to contemporary design that suggested Brigham as an exemplar of a hybrid approach to design and activism that has played out across the intervening century in ways not always reflected in histories of classic modernism in design. With a growing sense that Brigham's was a story worth telling in depth, my prolonged dive into her life and Progressive Era design history turned into this book. It has had all the characteristics of the best adventures you never meant to undertake: deeply engaging, full of surprises, more arduous than expected, and offering much food for thought along the way.

In terms of organization, this book mostly follows the chronology of Louise Brigham's life, although individual chapters are organized thematically around different aspects of her career. By way of an introduction, Chapter 1 places her on the island of Spitsbergen during a pivotal summer when she was working out her box furniture system. In considering what it took to bring a young, well-to-do Boston woman to this remote spot in 1906, the chapter begins to locate her in the broader context of Progressive Era art and design movements.

Chapter 2 traces her family background and patchy art education, especially her study of various arts and crafts in Europe and the important mentorship of Viennese designer Josef Hoffmann. It also examines her extended involvement with the settlement house movement in both the United States and Europe, focusing on how this may have shaped the early stages of her box furniture project, her commitment to design for the working class, and her later practices as an educator.

Chapter 3 is a close analysis of *Box Furniture*, the book Brigham published in 1909 about making furniture from recycled packing crates. It offers an overview of several overlapping aspects of Brigham's book, including the aesthetics of box furniture, her foregrounding of multifunctional and modular design, and her commitment to a do-it-yourself approach to furniture making. Her aesthetic is analyzed in terms of how it reflects the values of contemporary design movements, especially Arts and Crafts and Hoffmann's Wiener Werkstätte, and there is an examination of her work with the designer Edward H. Aschermann, who illustrated the book. Finally, there is a discussion of how the book fits into a burgeoning marketplace of advice writing and how box furniture aligned with the contemporary values of thrift and hygiene often promulgated by advice writers.

Chapter 4 turns to the social program underlying box furniture, focusing on the several channels through which Brigham publicized and advocated for box furniture apart from her book. In addition to writing magazine articles and giving talks, Brigham made a practice of furnishing her own New York apartments with box furniture and turning them into public showplaces for the aesthetic and social value of her project. Her holistic approach to the interior design of these apartments extended beyond her box furniture to items like linens that she herself designed and made, as well as wall treatments. Next, the chapter surveys the industrial expositions at which Brigham showed entire rooms of box furniture, placing both these exhibits and the showcase apartments as variants of the "model homes" that were a common feature of Progressive Era social projects.

Chapter 5 describes Brigham's efforts to train working-class children in carpentry through an organization she founded in New York City, the Home Thrift Association (HTA). In its ethos and goals, the HTA was aligned with skills-training organizations like the Home Arts and Industries Association in Great Britain and almost certainly drew on the tenets of the Scandinavian sloyd movement, with which Brigham had become familiar during her European travels.

Chapter 6 focuses on Brigham's attempts to commercialize her box furniture system. Around 1915, she founded the Home Art Masters company to manufacture and sell her I-Ma-Da line of ready-to-assemble (RTA) flat-pack furniture kits, an effort that was several decades ahead of the first really successful ventures into RTA furniture. In addition, toward the end of World War I she opened a school to train young women in carpentry, with an associated store where their products (especially toys) could be sold.

Chapter 7 assesses the period after World War I when Brigham's life changed direction and she slowly slid out of public view. Her marriage to retired Cleveland steel executive Henry Arnott Chisholm in 1916 may have factored into this transition, but it is also likely that her box furniture did not align well with the emerging values of convenience, ease, speed, and glamor that became design hallmarks of the 1920s. At some point, probably in the 1920s, Brigham worked on a planned 4th edition of her book *Box Furniture* that was never completed.

Chapter 8 surveys the period from the mid-1930s to the mid-1940s when Brigham became close to the healer and clairvoyant Edgar Cayce, his family, and his secretary Gladys Davis. Cayce gave Brigham a series of what he called "readings" on subjects ranging from her health to her supposed past lives, and these are examined closely for the details they reveal about her failing health, her financial situation, and especially her concern about her legacy as a designer and writer. Brigham's later-life turn toward the spiritual is also reflected in her brief association with Unity Church during World War II. The chapter concludes with her death in 1956.

Chapter 9 assesses Brigham as a progenitor of several strands of contemporary design, including sustainable and recycled-materials design, do-it-yourself design, modular and multifunctional design for apartments, and RTA and kit furniture design. Following an overview of how these areas of design developed over the last hundred years, the chapter takes up two examples of recent design projects to interrogate the ways in which contemporary design both reflects and diverges from Brigham's aesthetic and ethos. Finally, the chapter argues for Brigham as an exemplar of a form of "alternative modernity" that was radical for the unique ways that she took modernist ideas and refracted them through her own version of Progressive Era values.

As an aid to readers, the book includes a timeline of Brigham's life in the Appendix.

A difficulty of this project has been the scanty nature of primary materials on Brigham's life. Little in the way of personal documents and nothing in the way of original items of box furniture appear to have survived, possibly in part because Brigham had no direct descendants. It is my hope, however, that the light this book shines on her life may yet prompt new discoveries.

Long Beach, USA   Antoinette LaFarge

Acknowledgements

I am enormously grateful to the many people who have helped me bring this book to completion. I owe a special debt to the Institute of Cultural Inquiry for inviting me into its *100/10* residency project in 2011, where I first stumbled on Louise Brigham and her work; and likewise a debt to the Vermont Studio Center, which provided me with a residency in 2015 during which I wrote the first draft of Chapter 1.

For help with research, I am indebted to more people than I can reasonably thank here. Special thanks are owed to the staff of the Museum of the City of New York, especially Lindsay Turley, Lauren Robinson, and Emily Chapin; to Sarah Lewis, Emily Guthrie, and Lauri Perkins at the Winterthur Museum, Garden & Library; to Jessica Newell and Karen Davis at the Edgar Cayce Foundation; to Aurora McClain and Sidney Kirkpatrick for allowing me to use unpublished material from their own research; to Sharon Goodman and the membership of the Furniture History Society; to Heidi Voss-Nilsen at the Norsk Folkemuseum; to Jessica Pigza at the New York Public Library; to Chisholm Chandler and Rusty Chandler for information on the Chisholm family; to Diana Toole at Gracie Mansion; and to Cameron Hartnell for assistance with images. For reading drafts or sections of the manuscript and providing candid and useful feedback, I am profoundly grateful to Elizabeth Evitts Dickinson, Jesse Colin Jackson, and most of all to Lise Patt, whose wise comments helped me get through the last lap of revisions. Among these, too, I must count my anonymous peer reviewers, whose generous and thoughtful feedback was a great gift. Any errors that remain in the text must be laid at my door, not theirs.

As with all writing projects, the process has had its rough patches, and I am grateful to Maya Gurantz and Christel Dillbohner for kind encouragement, timely ideas, and good coffee along the way. Above all, I am grateful to Robert Allen for his unfailing support on this book as on all the journeys of our lives.

Long Beach, USA   Antoinette LaFarge

Contents

1	Introduction: Adventures of a Scrap Artist	1
2	The Limits of Education	13
3	Box Furniture	25
4	The Social Program	49
5	The Home Thrift Association	67
6	Ready-to-Assemble Furniture	77
7	Vanishing Act	85
8	Caycean Disciple	91
9	The Contemporary Context	99
Appendix: Timeline		113
Bibliography		117
Index		127

List of Figures

Fig. 1.1 Map of the Arctic Sea region with the Svalbard archipelago at upper left. Inset: central Spitsbergen showing Ice Fjord, where Louise Brigham spent two summers in the mining camp of Longyear City — 5

Fig. 1.2 Longyear City, 1906. The "portable house" is behind the left-hand tent (Photo courtesy of Anders B. Wilse/Norsk Folkemuseum) — 6

Fig. 1.3 Two pieces of Brigham's Spitsbergen box furniture, 1906: a sideboard (left) and hall stand (Photograph from Brigham's *Box Furniture*, 1909) — 7

Fig. 1.4 Some of Brigham's Spitsbergen tools. From Brigham's *Illustrated Lectures*, ca. 1914 (Photo courtesy of the Museum of the City of New York) — 8

Fig. 2.1 Louise Brigham, from her *Illustrated Lectures*, ca. 1914. The original photo was taken by Moffett of Chicago, Illinois (Photo courtesy of the Museum of the City of New York) — 14

Fig. 2.2 Austrian designer Josef Hoffmann, 1902 (Photo from Wikimedia Commons) — 18

Fig. 2.3 Brigham's monogram, from the back cover of her *Box Furniture*, 1909 — 19

Fig. 2.4 Sideboard at the Copenhagen settlement house, shown closed and open (From Brigham's *Box Furniture*, 1909) — 22

Fig. 3.1 The cover of the first edition of Brigham's *Box Furniture*, 1909 — 27

Fig. 3.2	Design for Brigham's quadruple writing desk (#41), with storage units serving as the legs. Shown here is the first of three pages of instructions for building this desk (From her *Box Furniture*, 1909)	28
Fig. 3.3	One of Brigham's larger pieces of Spitsbergen furniture, 1906: a combination desk, reading table, and bookcase with built-in lamps, constructed from packing crates (rear view) (Photograph from her *Box Furniture*, 1909)	30
Fig. 3.4	Brigham's Nest of Benches from her *Box Furniture*, 1909	36
Fig. 3.5	An ad for Globe Wernicke's "elastic" bookcases (Photo from Wikimedia Commons)	38
Fig. 3.6	Edward H. Aschermann's drawing of a dining room scheme for Brigham's *Box Furniture*, 1909	41
Fig. 3.7	An Edwardian living room, as published in *Ladies' Home Journal*, November 1, 1910, in an article immediately following Part III of Brigham's "How I Furnished My Entire Flat with Boxes"	43
Fig. 4.1	Drawing of Brigham's dining room furnished with box furniture, from the third installment of Brigham's article "How I Furnished My Entire Flat with Boxes" in *Ladies' Home Journal*, November 1, 1910 (Uncredited drawing, possibly by George A. Newman)	50
Fig. 4.2	Several possible configurations of the Greek-cross table both with and without its matching floor-based candlesticks, as published in *Ladies' Home Journal*, March 1910 (Image courtesy of HathiTrust, https://hdl.handle.net/2027/mdp.39015011414193)	51
Fig. 4.3	A drawing (possibly after a photograph) of the four sides of the living room at Box Corner First by George A. Newman, as published in *Ladies' Home Journal*, September 1, 1910 (Image courtesy of HathiTrust, https://hdl.handle.net/2027/mdp.39015011414193)	52
Fig. 4.4	Brigham design for bookcase with double doors, as published in *Ladies' Home Journal*, September 1, 1910 (Image courtesy of HathiTrust, https://hdl.handle.net/2027/mdp.39015011414193)	53
Fig. 4.5	Brigham design for a combination writing desk (with portfolio case) and file cabinet, as published in *Ladies' Home Journal*, September 1, 1910. This design is not included in Brigham's *Box Furniture* (Image courtesy of HathiTrust, https://hdl.handle.net/2027/mdp.39015011414193)	54

Fig. 4.6	The living room at Box Corner Second, as published in Brigham's *Illustrated Lectures,* ca. 1914. Designs for the large armchair at left and the combination table-bookcase at center are not included in Brigham's *Box Furniture.* The pair of smaller chairs could be Brigham's Desk Chair (#40) with padding (Photo courtesy of the Museum of the City of New York)	57
Fig. 4.7	The box furniture corner seat at Box Corner Third, as shown in *Illustrated Lectures,* ca. 1914. At the right-hand end is the multifunctional Week-End Cabinet. This design is not included in Brigham's *Box Furniture* (Photo courtesy of the Museum of the City of New York)	58
Fig. 4.8	A model room of box furniture at a Child Welfare Exhibit, New York, 1911, as published in *Illustrated Lectures,* ca. 1914 (Photo courtesy of the Museum of the City of New York)	59
Fig. 4.9	A model room of box furniture at the Women's Industrial Exposition, Grand Central Palace, New York, 1912, as published in Brigham's *Illustrated Lectures,* ca. 1914 (Photo courtesy of the Museum of the City of New York)	60
Fig. 5.1	HTA boy with lumber from dismantled packing crates, sorted by size. From "Making Box Furniture" in *The Craftsman,* November 1911 (Image courtesy of HathiTrust, http://hdl.handle.net/2027/gri.ark:/13960/t17m7c85n)	69
Fig. 5.2	Home Thrift Association boys taking home completed furniture (Photo courtesy of the Museum of the City of New York)	70
Fig. 5.3	HTA boys camping with Tak-Apart Furniture. From Brigham's *Illustrated Lectures,* ca. 1914. Original photo credited to Brown Brothers (Photo courtesy of the Museum of the City of New York)	72
Fig. 6.1	An ad for Home Art Masters kit furniture in *The Masses,* July 1915 (Image courtesy of HathiTrust and the Labadie Collection at the University of Michigan)	80
Fig. 7.1	Brigham's annotated list of tool changes in a copy of the 1919 edition of *Box Furniture* (Photo courtesy of the Winterthur Library: Printed Book and Periodical Collection)	86
Fig. 8.1	Healer and clairvoyant Edgar Cayce, 1941 (Photo courtesy of Edgar Cayce Foundation)	92
Fig. 8.2	Louise Brigham (center) with Edgar Cayce's son Hugh Lynn Cayce (left) and Hugh's wife Sally (right), 1941 (Photo courtesy of Edgar Cayce Foundation)	97

Fig. 9.1	Gerrit Rietveld's Crate Chair, ca. 1934 (Photo courtesy of Brooklyn Museum, gift of Rosemarie Haag Bletter and Martin Filler, 1994.160. Creative Commons-BY [Photo: Brooklyn Museum, CUR.1994.160.jpg])	101
Fig. 9.2	A detail of Van Bo Le-Mentzel's schematic for version 3 of his 24-Euro Chair (Image courtesy of the artist)	104
Fig. 9.3	Farah Nasser's rendering of her multifunctional furniture designs, 2013 (Image courtesy of the artist)	105

CHAPTER 1

Introduction: Adventures of a Scrap Artist

Abstract The Progressive Era designer and social activist Louise Brigham spent a pivotal summer on the far-northern island of Spitsbergen in the early 1900s developing her system for building box furniture out of recycled packing crates. This chapter considers how a young, well-to-do Boston woman came to be in this remote spot in 1906 (then known to Europeans mainly as a jumping-off point for polar exploration), what life was like in the Arctic Coal Company mining camp where she stayed, and how she went about her work there. Following this is an examination of how women like Brigham came to be largely written out of standard histories of design through a combination of gender bias and devaluation of the social aspects of design that were prominent in Brigham's box furniture project.

Keywords Louise Brigham · Spitsbergen · Box furniture · Arctic Coal Company

"Two summers on the island of Spitzbergen," wrote the Progressive Era designer Louise Brigham in 1909, "taught me, more than all previous experiments, the latent possibilities of a box."[1] The book she published that year, *Box Furniture*, is indeed a testament to the possibilities of a box—and not just any box, but specifically the packing crates then used to ship all kinds of ordinary consumer goods. Brigham found in those

© The Author(s) 2019
A. LaFarge, *Louise Brigham and the Early History of Sustainable Furniture Design*,
https://doi.org/10.1007/978-3-030-32341-7_1

humble, cheaply made boxes inspiration for a unique system of furniture design based entirely on recycled packing crates.

The first of those two summers was 1906. The American journalist and explorer Walter Wellman had set up headquarters on Danes Island in the Svalbard archipelago, more than 800 miles above the Arctic Circle. From there he would launch several attempts to reach the North Pole by dirigible. He failed in these (as in several later ones), his efforts thwarted by a combination of bad planning and mechanical failures. He will nonetheless be counted among a haloed group of late nineteenth and early twentieth century Arctic and Antarctic adventurers: Salomon Andrée, Umberto Nobile, Ernest Shackleton, Roald Amundsen—all of whom also launched expeditions from the northern fringe of Svalbard. Wellman's grandiosity marks him as a devotee of what has been termed the "polar imaginary," a field for the inscriptions of ambitious men, regardless of whether they set out for the frigid zones in person or, like the artist Frederic Church, set down their visions of the icy sublime in paint.

That summer of 1906, members of Wellman's team met a quite different sort of American adventurer: Louise Brigham, who was spending a few months on Spitsbergen, Svalbard's largest island. It was an odd place for a young woman from Boston to find herself, even given the fact that well-to-do New Englanders of the period often took a puritanical attitude toward their vacations, believing that moral fiber would be developed through privation and physical challenge. Brigham was 31 that summer and single; her parents were long dead. She was there with friends, but in certain essential ways, she was also alone: there was no family to offer comfort and support, no cohort of competitors to drive her on, no band of women to normalize her presence. Her peers were mostly at home, many of them already married and raising children. So her presence in this Norwegian outpost on the edge of the Arctic Ocean suggests a person of some courage and imagination. When Louise returns to the United States, it will be with none of the glamor and acclaim that attended Wellman and the other Arctic explorers of the day. Yet during this sojourn, she explored and developed an idea whose legacy is still playing out today, even though Brigham herself is all but unknown.

Louise Brigham came home from that summer on Spitsbergen to develop an entire program for building furniture out of salvaged packing crates. She wrote out her ideas in the book *Box Furniture*, which made her briefly famous. She championed this system as an economical way for the working poor to afford good design, as a way of reskilling city dwellers, and as a shining example of American thriftiness. She also started a mail-order business to sell kits of ready-to-assemble (RTA) furniture direct to consumers. In all of these activities, she exemplified the Progressive Era ethos while still pushing ahead of her contemporaries on a number of fronts. Her aesthetic was rough-hewn and starkly rectilinear at a time when the reigning styles were versions of elegant simplicity: Art Nouveau and its Germanic counterpart Jugendstil, the American Craftsman and Prairie School styles, the Vienna Secession. In certain respects, her work anticipates by a decade the plainer geometries of De Stijl, and it will be nearly three decades before furniture based on recycled materials enters the realm of high design through Dutch De Stijl designer Gerrit Rietveld's Crate Chair.[2] Her mail-order furniture kits represent a rare step toward an industry that would not take off until the late 1940s. And today, several prominent areas of contemporary design trace directly back to, or through, Brigham's project: especially recycled-materials design, low-impact design, do-it-yourself design, multifunctional design, and modular design. In her commitment to an open practice and craftsmanship by amateurs, she has a great deal in common with the open source movement in design. Indeed, it would not be too much to call her a progenitor of the sustainable design movement.

To understand Louise Brigham, we must begin by delving further into that first summer on Spitsbergen. The island's name—"pointed mountains" in Dutch—neatly describes its geology. Roughly triangular, about 100 miles wide by 150 long, it is so riven by fjords that it resembles a giant piece of rocky lace. In summer, when Brigham was there, it warms up to around 40 degrees Fahrenheit and is often foggy. From the seventeenth to the nineteenth century it was visited mainly by fur hunters and whalers, the latter of whom might do a little opportunistic coal mining on the side. The major nation-states of the northern hemisphere considered Svalbard *terra nullius*—no one's land, open for exploitation by all and un-ownable by any—but that tacit agreement began to fray during the heyday of European whaling and would be erased by the Svalbard Treaty of 1920.[3] Toward the end of the nineteenth century, coal mining began in earnest and has since remained one of Spitsbergen's main industries (lately supplemented by tourism and scientific research).

One of the island's first large-scale mining developers was John Munro Longyear, a Minnesotan who had already made a fortune on mining claims in the Lake Superior region before he formed a partnership to buy land claims on Spitsbergen beginning in 1904.[4] (On the scale of wealth, John

Munro Longyear existed in a universe where he could dismantle a mansion he had built in Wisconsin, transship its pieces 1300 miles to eastern Massachusetts, and rebuild it even larger—a feat so extreme in its day that it made it into *Ripley's Believe It Or Not*.)[5] By 1906, Longyear and his partner had established the Arctic Coal Company to mine claims on Ice Fjord, which cuts deep into the west coast of Spitsbergen, nearly bisecting the island. Longyear made his nephew, William Dearborn Munroe, the company's general manager.[6] Brigham arrived on Spitsbergen aboard Longyear's yacht as a guest of Munroe and as a companion for his wife, prepared to spend the summer in the newly founded mining camp on Arctic Coal Company Tract No. 1.[7] Located in a small valley on the south shore of Ice Fjord, at the foot of one of its many finger bays, the camp was then known by the glorified title of Longyear City and today is called Longyearbyen (Fig. 1.1).

A century later, Longyearbyen is the largest settlement in the archipelago, with a population hovering around 2000 people. When Brigham was there, however, its population consisted mainly of Svalbard reindeer, Arctic foxes, and migratory seabirds, accented by a few isolated clumps of coal miners. Polar bears, too, abound on Spitsbergen—it is not by chance that Philip Pullman features them so prominently in the Svalbard episodes of his trilogy of novels entitled *His Dark Materials*. Conditions were extremely primitive in Longyear City, which housed about 80 men at the time of Brigham's 1906 visit. There was no electricity: the camp's powerhouse wouldn't be built for another three years. There was no regular water supply. All food and equipment had to be brought in by ship during the summer months—the nearest transshipment point was over 530 miles southeast, in Hammerfest, Norway—and stockpiled to supply the camp during the eight months it would be cut off from the outside world by winter ice. There were no roads, only footpaths, and anything arriving at the Advent Bay dock had to be brought the half-mile up to the camp by human labor—in July 1906, a narrow-gauge railway to link camp and dock was still in the planning stage.[8]

In a 1906 photograph, the camp amounts to little more than a loose cluster of tents, a few sheds, and a handful of wooden buildings. The most impressive of these were a large, abandoned Norwegian tourist cabin that had been converted to living quarters for the miners (it would later become the company store), and the one-and-a-half story, eight-room "portable house" where Brigham and the Munroes lived (Fig. 1.2).[9] It was sparsely furnished, and Brigham quickly decided to see what she could do to make

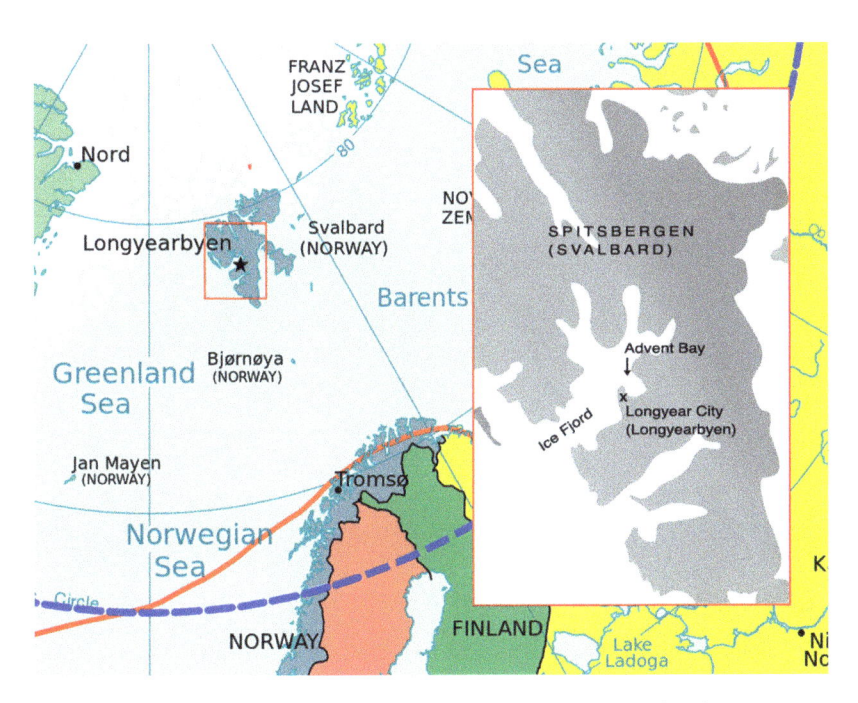

Fig. 1.1 Map of the Arctic Sea region with the Svalbard archipelago at upper left. Inset: central Spitsbergen showing Ice Fjord, where Louise Brigham spent two summers in the mining camp of Longyear City

living conditions more bearable by constructing some furniture. That she had both the ambition and the expertise to undertake this project is rather remarkable. Girls of the day were ordinarily trained only in the tools suitable for "womanly" occupations like sewing, needlework, and basketry. Already by the late nineteenth century, feminists were arguing that girls just as much as boys ought to be taught to use hammers and saws, but they hadn't yet made much headway.[10] Brigham, however, was a trained artist who had skills with tools that went right back to her New England girlhood.[11] Throughout her 20s and 30s, she went to some lengths to develop these skills, and as we will see, she would later take care to teach them to others.

The stacks of leftover boxes on Spitsbergen prompted Brigham to continue some earlier experiments she had made in building furniture out of scrap wood. Perhaps the crucial factor pushing her to move forward was the bare fact that there was no other source of wood on Spitsbergen. As

Fig. 1.2 Longyear City, 1906. The "portable house" is behind the left-hand tent (Photo courtesy of Anders B. Wilse/Norsk Folkemuseum)

Brigham wryly observed a few years later, the sole local 'tree' was the polar willow, *Salix polaris*, a dwarf shrub that grows only a few inches tall.[12] Out of the canned-goods boxes stacked around the camp, Brigham built an assortment of furniture. The few surviving photographs of the camp interiors inform us that there were a desk, a sideboard, a hall stand, and some shelves; there were undoubtedly also tables and chairs (Fig. 1.3).

Although 1906 was clearly a transformational summer, Brigham goes short on specifics in her own accounts of what she did at Longyear City. She writes about her Svalbard summers—she would return the following year[13]—with a maddening combination of cheeriness and reticence. Precisely at the point in her accounts where the reader is hoping for vivid details about the making of her box furniture, she transitions into vague generalities: "As I worked in that far-off marvelous land of continuous day, surrounded by mountains and glaciers, I felt anew the truth, so familiar to all, that work to be of real value must be honest, useful, and beautiful."[14]

Fig. 1.3 Two pieces of Brigham's Spitsbergen box furniture, 1906: a sideboard (left) and hall stand (Photograph from Brigham's *Box Furniture*, 1909)

(There is an echo here of William Morris's admonition: "Have nothing in your house that you do not know to be useful or believe to be beautiful.")[15]

That's all very well, but what one really wants to know are the nitty-gritty details. What kind of difficulties did Brigham encounter trying to make furniture under mining-camp conditions, with the hand tools of the day? In a photograph showing the tools she used that summer, it's possible to make out a file, a carpenter's plane, a large two-handed brace-and-bit for drilling, and possibly a hacksaw as well (Fig. 1.4). Did she have a good workspace; did her packing crates get destroyed by rain; did she throw her hammer at the wall in frustration? How did her design ideas mature through the process of experimentation? Did she long to quit and go back home? (Which might have been impossible in any case, as even in summer,

Fig. 1.4 Some of Brigham's Spitsbergen tools. From Brigham's *Illustrated Lectures*, ca. 1914 (Photo courtesy of the Museum of the City of New York)

the Longyear yacht was apparently icebound.)[16] Was she mocked, cheered, ignored by the camp's other—mostly male—residents?

This last question is the only one we can answer, at least nominally. Sometime that summer, members of Walter Wellman's team traveled the hundred or so miles south from Danes Island to Longyear City.[17] On inspecting the portable house with its reconstructed-box furnishings, one of the Wellman team told Mrs. Longyear that she had the "northernmost civilized home in the world"—praise indeed, but likewise a reduction of Brigham's woodworking skills and design ingenuity to the 'natural' and 'feminine' role of homemaking. When compared with a complicated expedition to a hyped-up point of global geometry—the typical goal of polar expeditions then and now—Brigham's accomplishment can easily be made to look rather small. Spun as domestic economy, Brigham's project on Spitsbergen can be written off as yet another form of the endless drudge work done by women. But considered instead as life-support engineering or as minimal-impact design, it's another matter altogether. What Brigham did was think carefully about what it would take to sustain and even improve life under tough conditions with very, very limited resources. While Wellman's team, like the other expeditions of the day, was leaving refuse strewn over hundreds of miles of terrain, Brigham's "inventive genius"[18] was putting camp waste to use. Among the questions that the Spitsbergen summer leaves open are: How did it come about that Brigham could make of this curious sojourn a turning point in her adult life? And how is it that her unique design project came to be all but forgotten?

It has been widely observed that histories of design persistently omit women or devalue their design-related activities as either superfluous decoration (under the catchall term "crafts") or uncreative practical activities.[19] There is a concomitant essentialization of certain qualities, mediums, and skills as "feminine" and therefore a priori of less value. As ever more gendered spheres developed under industrial capitalism starting in the late eighteenth century—the domestic female sphere where women's labor was assumed to be free, and the public male sphere where men's labor was paid—the result was a socially reified distinction between "amateur women" and "professional men."[20] Louise Brigham was born into a world where "professional women" barely existed as a category, and her career bears witness to her persistence in making opportunities for herself within those constraints. Yet insofar as furniture design history has been largely a study of mass-produced, highly refined, and often expensive objects designed by professional men, Brigham's project of individually made, materially crude pieces of furniture designed for working people by a nonprofessional woman was almost categorically bound to be excluded or dismissed under the label of eccentricity. Writing about the home industries movement in England—which arose in the 1880s to preserve and teach vanishing traditional handicrafts—William Morris's biographer J. W. Mackail observed that it was "a mixture of charity and patronage [that served to] multiply the production of amateur incompetency."[21] That harsh judgment could just as easily be used to sweep away Brigham's box furniture and the young men she trained to make it.

It is also the case that Brigham's valuation of the social aspects of box furniture as at least co-equal to the aesthetic aspect put her out of synch with the ways in which design history has been written. If there has been a tendency among historians to elide the radical ideas championed by William Morris as a kind of armchair socialism and focus on the formal excellence of his design work, how much more would that not be the case with someone like Brigham? This book, then, is an attempt to reimagine Brigham's work as an exemplar of a specific approach to design, one that foregrounds the "ingenuity, enterprise and self reliance" that Clive Edwards argues has characterized women's making for many centuries.[22] It positions her at a moment when modern design was struggling to take new forms in the United States during the first two decades of the twentieth century, and Progressives like Brigham were involved in trying not solely to shape style and taste but also to connect design to a social mission. In particular, it argues for Brigham as someone who placed social practice as the driver of aesthetics and thereby envisioned a world in which good design is understood as reflecting the values of reuse over novelty, a communitarian approach over individual genius, and a do-it-yourself ethos over mass production.

Notes

1. Brigham, *Box Furniture*, Preface, 1. Brigham herself does not give dates for the two summers she spent on Spitsbergen in any sources I have found. The Walter Wellman meeting and other evidence from histories of Spitsbergen make it clear she was there in 1906 and again in 1907. See, e.g., Hartnell, "Arctic Network Builders," 51–75. Throughout this book, I am using the more usual 'Spitsbergen' spelling rather than Brigham's 'Spitzbergen' except in direct quotations.
2. See, for example, Attfield, "What Does History Have to Do with It?," 78.
3. Hartnell, "Arctic Network Builders," 41.
4. For a full acount of Longyear's mining enterprise on Spitsbergen, see Hartnell, "Arctic Network Builders."
5. Longyear's wife, Mary Beecher Longyear, was a philanthropist who would become known a few years later for funding the first Braille version of the King James Bible.
6. Some sources, including Louise Brigham, list Munroe as Longyear's cousin. I rely here on two well-researched histories of coal mining on Spitsbergen: Hartnell, "Arctic Network Builders," 65; Dole, *America in Spitsbergen*.
7. Hartnell, "Arctic Network Builders," 75; "Louise Chisholm, Crafts Expert, 81," 15. The latter (Brigham's obituary in the *New York Times*) mistakenly states that Brigham was "wintering" on Spitsbergen.
8. Hartnell, "Arctic Network Builders," 126–128 and 137–140. That half-mile was a best-case scenario, too: in early summer, the first ship of the year might not get any closer than 30 miles away.

9. It is unclear what Brigham means by portable house, but it was likely a wooden building brought in sections to Spitsbergen and erected on site. It was replaced a year or two later with a permanent building for mining company staff.
10. Gelber, *Hobbies*, 212.
11. Brigham later remarked that as a child she had not cared much for tools but because she was interested in anything that could be done with the hands, she learned how to use the basic tools: hammer and saw, chisel and square. "Making Box Furniture," 218. Also, Gelber, *Hobbies*, 212.
12. Brigham, *Box Furniture*, Preface, 2.
13. Hartnell, "Arctic Network Builders," 181. It's not clear why she would have returned in 1907 when William Munroe, the person who brought her there originally, died in the sinking of the S. S. Berlin off Holland in February 1907.
14. Brigham, *Box Furniture*, Preface, 2.
15. Morris, "Beauty of Life," 561.
16. "Louise Chisholm, Crafts Expert," 15.
17. Apparently the Prince of Monaco also visited Brigham's house that summer and was equally pleased by it. Brigham, *Box Furniture*, Preface, 3.
18. "Guide to the New Books," 207.
19. On this subject, see, for example, Kirkham, *Women Designers*; Buckley, "Made in Patriarchy"; Parker, *Subversive Stitch*; Edwards, "Home Is Where the Art Is"; and Mancini, *Pre-modernism*.
20. Edwards, "Home Is Where the Art Is," 11.
21. Harrod, *Real Thing*, 316.
22. Edwards, "Home Is Where the Art Is," 19.

CHAPTER 2

The Limits of Education

Abstract This chapter traces the family background and patchy art education of Progressive Era designer and social activist Louise Brigham, especially her study of various arts and crafts in Europe and the important mentorship of Viennese designer Josef Hoffmann. There is a consideration of the limitations of design education for women of her generation, as well as the difficulty of establishing professional careers. The chapter also examines her extended involvement with the settlement movement in New York City and Cleveland, Ohio, as well as in Copenhagen, Denmark, focusing on how this may have shaped the early stages of her box furniture project, her commitment to design for the working class, and her later practices as an educator.

Keywords Louise Brigham · Box furniture · Josef Hoffmann · Settlement movement · Design education

Louise Ashton Brigham (1875–1956) was born to William Cleveland Brigham, an apothecary in Medford, Massachusetts, and Maria Wilson Sheppard Brigham.[1] She was the fourth of five children, with one brother, Waldo, and two surviving sisters, Lucy and Anna Esther. As an adult, Brigham stood five feet four inches tall at full growth and was of medium

© The Author(s) 2019
A. LaFarge, *Louise Brigham and the Early History of Sustainable Furniture Design*,
https://doi.org/10.1007/978-3-030-32341-7_2

Fig. 2.1 Louise Brigham, from her *Illustrated Lectures*, ca. 1914. The original photo was taken by Moffett of Chicago, Illinois (Photo courtesy of the Museum of the City of New York)

build with fair skin and blue eyes. Like most adult women of the Edwardian era, she wore her long brown hair in a conventional chignon (Fig. 2.1).

Little is known about her father's family, but on her mother's side, Brigham descended from an English family, the Merriams, who had been in Massachusetts since the early seventeenth century, mostly as farmers and small businessmen.[2] Brigham's mother died when she was just two, so she was probably raised in large part by relatives or servants—nannies or governesses. There is ample evidence to suggest that Brigham was born into reasonably affluent circumstances and that she very likely gained an inheritance when her father died in 1894. Brigham never had to work for a living, she was able to travel extensively throughout her life, and she came to own several apartments in New York City. Perhaps most tellingly, between her father's death when she was in her late teens and her marriage at the age of 41, she was apparently not supported by an adult male relative, as was usual for single women in this period. Moreover, she was able to take advantage of college-level study at a time when less than 10% of Americans even graduated from high school.

Sometime in the mid-1890s—possibly after her father's death—she moved to New York, where she studied at some of the most advanced art schools of the period. She briefly attended the Chase School of Art (which became the New York School of Art in 1898 and is known today as Parsons The New School for Design)[3] before moving over to the Pratt Institute. In this period toward the end of the nineteenth century, design was still largely a male field.[4] At the same time, in no small part thanks to the efforts of first-wave feminists, ambitious middle-class American women were beginning to demand full access to professions that had heretofore been closed to them, and to the training that would allow them to enter those professions. Several major design schools—the New York School of Design for Women (a forerunner of Cooper Union), the Philadelphia School of Design for Women, the Western Reserve School of Design (a forerunner of the Cleveland Institute of Art)—were founded in the second half of the nineteenth century by women as a way to ensure respectable work for women like Louise Brigham.[5]

This represented a major shift from just a generation or two earlier. As women gained more leisure time throughout the nineteenth century, a kind of domestic segregation had begun to be imagined and then enforced. The home became women's realm, while the world of (real, paid) work belonged to men.[6] Accompanying this was a push to route women's skills away from the necessities of daily life (like clothes-making) and into decorative work that would keep them from the sin of idleness while also keeping them from competing with men in the market.[7] For such women, doing paid professional work was a sign of lower (or lost) social status, further solidifying the pernicious idea that the only acceptable work for women was a form of unpaid service to family or society.[8] At the height of this period in the Victorian era, middle-class women used their ingenuity to transform small materials into "fancy work," creating ornamental objects out of feathers, butterfly wings, seeds, porcupine quills, seashells, colored sand, pine cones, and human hair, as well as the more traditional paint and embroidery. They weren't encouraged to use anything much heavier than cardboard because materials like wood and plaster—let alone the tools to work with such materials—were considered unsuitable for women's "delicate and dainty fingers."[9]

It was only in the last couple decades of the nineteenth century that a few advanced thinkers like the educator Catherine Beecher called for women to be given hammers and saws, files, chisels, screwdrivers, gimlets, and drills. As the century turned over, encouraging women to become skilled in the design arts began to be seen as a good way to keep them out of the political sphere, where the suffrage and Progressive movements were gaining momentum. Yet even with professional training, women designers faced some major career obstacles. For one thing, they could generally develop their design careers only if they worked as an assistant to a male designer and/or married a designer—it was extremely difficult for them to establish careers on their own. Moreover, women designers were steered toward fields that by this time had been tagged as feminine or domestic, such as embroidery, china painting, lacemaking, simple jewelry, and later interior design.[10] In other words, they got out from the Victorian cage of fancy work's "monstrous masterpieces"[11] only to find themselves in the slightly expanded cage of domestic arts. At the same time, we can see a pattern in the lives of women of this era in the way they combined activities in several different fields—the arts plus education, say, or the arts plus philanthropy—to create a viable public life for themselves.

While attending the New York art schools, Brigham was certainly exposed to some of the art magazines that had begun appearing in the immediately preceding decades as part of a magazine publication boom, such as *The American Art Review, Fine Arts, The Art Journal, The Art Worker, The Art Student, The Art Age, The American Art Printer*, and perhaps especially *Modern Art*, which championed vanguardist American artists in the 1890s.[12] Several of these magazines, including *Art Interchange* and *Art Amateur*, made a point of featuring work by women artists.[13] Brigham also likely saw the very popular and commercially successful exhibitions put on by the New York Society for Decorative Art, which had been founded in 1877 by the artist Candace Wheeler.

But Brigham only attended the New York schools for a few years, and it is likely that she acquired most of her design education—both practical skills and advanced ideas—by another route, one open only to women of her social class. She decided to train in various art-making and craft techniques by going to Europe and studying there. From the late 1900s well into the twentieth century, this kind of European trip was standard practice for upper middle-class British and American artists.[14] As Brigham put it in an interview some years later: "I spent the biggest part of five years in Europe, studying various kinds of handiwork with the peasants and the artists of nineteen different countries."[15] It is difficult to date these travels with any certainty, as Brigham tended to refer to them offhandedly in later interviews. They must fall in the decade between about 1897, when she left art school, and 1910, when she starts mentioning them in interviews. She was much occupied with the settlement movement in the early years of this period, so the likeliest time frame for her travels would be between 1904 and 1909, give or take a year or two at either end; the two summers on Spitsbergen thus fall toward the middle of this period.

Brigham went to Sweden to study advanced wood-carving at the Sloyd Institute in Naas (an experience that was undoubtedly influential on her later decision to open a carpentry training workshop), and then to Copenhagen to continue her woodworking studies at the National Industrial School. She made a stop at the National Art School in Haarlem, Holland, and she met with the architect and furniture designer Charles Rennie Mackintosh in Glasgow. There were other encounters with master teachers in Christiana, Dresden, Berlin, Paris, London, and Coburg from whom she picked up techniques in weaving, spinning, dyeing, basketry, and metalwork.[16]

It is evident that Brigham focused on industrial design arts in ways that fed her box furniture project: notably woodworking, wood-carving, and furniture design (as well as weaving, which could be put to use for cushions and curtains). She made a number of friends along the way, including the Swedish painter Carl Larsson and his wife, the artist-designer Karin Larsson.[17] The design historian Neville Thompson thinks it likely that Karin Larsson's own furniture designs may have had an influence on Brigham's later work, and certainly the Larssons' preference for simpler furniture and folk-art-inspired textiles was very close to Brigham's own aesthetic.[18] In any case, it is likely that Brigham was looking not just for an education but for a mentor, without whom it was very difficult for women of the day to function in the public sphere. So the most important of these encounters was undoubtedly with Josef Hoffmann, a professor at the Vienna Kunstgewerbeschule (School of Applied Arts) (Fig. 2.2).

Hoffmann, who became Brigham's friend as well as a mentor, was an Austrian architect and designer who was just five years older than Brigham. He is considered one of the cofounders (in 1897) of the Vienna Secession—a movement to displace historicism in architecture in favor of lighter and more geometric forms—and of the Wiener Werkstätte (in 1903), a

Fig. 2.2 Austrian designer Josef Hoffmann, 1902 (Photo from Wikimedia Commons)

loose confederation of artists and designers who took a holistic and at times playful view of design and who worked with a highly stylized visual vocabulary. Hoffmann's own furniture and tableware designs are elegant, their spare geometric forms often modulated by the use of rounded corners and curves. Many of Hoffmann's designs riff on the square, a motif that Brigham would later acknowledge as the inspiration for her own design

Fig. 2.3 Brigham's monogram, from the back cover of her *Box Furniture*, 1909

aesthetic. She pays homage to Hoffmann's square for her own monogram of a squared-off B nested inside the angle of a squarish capital L, all within a square frame (Fig. 2.3).[19] Brigham's box furniture would ultimately rely on the rectangle as its base unit rather than the square, but her systematizing approach to design as well as her commitment to rectilinear form was likely influenced by Hoffmann and the Wiener Werkstätte.

During her time with Hoffmann, Brigham may have visited the Wiener Werkstätte showroom (it opened in 1904) or seen some of his students' work at one of the annual Secession shows. Either way, she would have become familiar with the group's emphasis on treating all elements of an interior as part of an integrated whole. This could be one source of her own holistic approach to box furniture design (other sources might include Charles Rennie Mackintosh or Frank Lloyd Wright). She might also have been drawn to the way Hoffmann and his students drew on folk art motifs for their designs of such items as textiles and tableware.[20]

Another important element in Brigham's education was her involvement with the American settlement movement, which aimed to set up group housing where middle-class people would live with, and help to educate, their working-class (often immigrant) neighbors.[21] Ultimately, more than a hundred settlement houses were established across the United States, some of which included training in forms of handiwork that could allow working-class women to earn an independent living. This was also seen as a way of preserving and passing on traditional crafts brought to the United States by immigrants, skills and knowledge that might otherwise be lost forever. This mix of "charity and design,"[22] underpinned by an idea that art could be socially redemptive, would have appealed strongly to Brigham and undoubtedly informed her later box furniture project.

In the mid-1890s, when Brigham transferred from the Chase School of Art in New York to the Pratt Institute in Brooklyn, she had won a scholarship and changed the focus of her studies. She began taking courses in the Domestic Art, Domestic Science, and Kindergarten departments,[23] the latter of which was known for teaching with Froebel toys[24]—and it's certainly possible that those Froebel toys that consisted of small wooden geometric units indirectly influenced her later reliance on blocklike elements in her furniture design.[25] Brigham also became involved with the Pratt Institute Neighborship Association and its residential Neighborship Settlement in the Astral Apartment building in Greenpoint, Brooklyn. In the summer of 1897 or 1898, Brigham had charge of a children's playground at the Neighborship Settlement and was also tasked with teaching millinery and cooking classes.[26] She later said of herself that she spent some thirteen years altogether as a social worker in New York.[27] In her 1905 passport application, she describes her occupation as "settlement worker."

In the early 1900s, Brigham extended her involvement with the settlement movement by joining a team attempting to set up settlement houses in Cleveland, Ohio. She provided the funds to create a settlement house in an immigrant neighborhood of Cleveland; it was named Sunshine Cottage because "it was meant to be a bright spot in a dark street."[28] Here, sharing the house with "a deserted scrub woman and her child,"[29] she apparently carried out her earliest real experiments in building furniture out of recycled materials "as a useful amusement."[30] Her first piece was, appropriately enough, a child's high chair.[31]

In April of 1905—just a year before her first summer on Spitsbergen—Brigham gave a talk about the Sunshine Cottage project to the monthly meeting of the New York Charity Organization Society. She stressed how her aim with the Sunshine Cottage had been "to demonstrate the fact that low-rental houses can be furnished practically, artistically, and yet cheaply."[32] The sideboard of the Sunshine Cottage, a set of nested benches,[33] "and many other useful articles" were made from empty boxes, for a total cost of $148.02 to furnish the ten-room cottage. With a cost more than ten times what it would later be, it is evident that she had not yet gotten very far with the thrift side of things. Nor was the aesthetic program at all in place. There are cheesecloth curtains in place of later tight-woven cotton or linen equivalents. There are sadly untransformed broom-handle curtain rods. Most of all, according to Brigham's own account, there is what sounds like a surplus of brown: brown dados and brown tablecloths and brown chair-rails from which hung brown kitchen utensils.[34] Edward H. Aschermann, the designer who would later illustrate Brigham's book on *Box Furniture*, inveighed against drab color palettes like this, and this is almost the last we will see of them in her career.[35]

Brigham remained in Cleveland working with the settlement movement until she came down with typhoid fever. It was on her recovery that she decided to continue her education in Europe, with an eye to learning more about "the art of frugality."[36] Her goal then was to establish more cottages on her eventual return to the United States.[37] In Copenhagen in 1907, her settlement work and nascent box furniture ideas came together in a more developed way when she oversaw university students in furnishing a club room in a settlement house with items constructed from salvaged boxes. Among these were a game table, a massive sideboard, a china cabinet, and a large corner seat. Designs for several of these would appear in Brigham's 1909 book *Box Furniture*, including the Game table (#56), the Copenhagen Sideboard (#86; Fig. 2.4), and the Club-room Corner Seat (#99).[38]

It was not uncommon for women involved with the settlement movement to extend their activities into such areas as design, architecture, and housing, taking advantage of the fact that activities from which they were

Fig. 2.4 Sideboard at the Copenhagen settlement house, shown closed and open (From Brigham's *Box Furniture*, 1909)

professionally barred might be countenanced under the umbrella of philanthropy.[39] In this respect, Brigham's designs of furniture for the settlement houses in Cleveland and Copenhagen fits into an existing pattern. It was also not uncommon for women who worked in settlement houses to also write domestic advice books. For example, the writer Martha Bensley Bruere worked at Hull House in Chicago and in the first couple decades of the twentieth century wrote about household matters in various magazines like *Good Housekeeping*.[40] Women like Bruere may have been role models for Brigham when she came to write her book about box furniture, the summation of her experiments in Cleveland, Longyear City, and Copenhagen.

Notes

1. William Cleveland Brigham (1840–1894) and Maria Wilson Sheppard Brigham (1845–1877) had five children; for details see the Appendix. Louise was the second youngest of the four girls and one boy. Pope et al., in *Merriam Genealogy in England and America* (108), give Brigham's first name

as "Louisa"; it's uncertain if this is technically correct, but in any case she used Louise her entire life.
2. Pope, *Merriam Genealogy*, 108.
3. "Louise Chisholm, Crafts Expert," 15. It is unclear if Brigham ever earned a degree from either school. According to librarian Emily Guthrie at the Winterthur Museum, Library & Garden (personal communication), design historian Neville Thompson discovered from a Pratt Institute librarian that Brigham's name does not appear on Pratt's list of graduates.
4. Attfield, "What Does History Have to Do with It?," 22; Aynsley and Berry, "Publishing the Modern Home," 3.
5. Kirkham, *Women Designers*, 50–51.
6. Kardon, *Ideal Home*, 32.
7. For more on the limitations imposed on women's skills in this period, see Gelber, *Hobbies*, 155–182; Parker, *Subversive Stitch*, 5–11.
8. Adamson, *Thinking Through Craft*, 140.
9. Gelber, *Hobbies*, 168. Note that the picture would probably have been rather different for women with less leisure, such as women living on the western frontier, or women without male family members to call on. They might very well have been conversant with carpentry tools; however it remains the case that they wouldn't have been able to gain that knowledge through ordinary educational channels. Indeed, debates about whether girls should be taught woodworking in school continued in the United States for decades after Brigham's day.
10. Kirkham, *Women Designers*, 51, 62; Lees-Maffei, "Professionalization."
11. Gelber, *Hobbies*, 193.
12. For more on this boom, see Mancini, *Pre-modernism*, 17–36, 62; Ferry, "Introduction," 22.
13. Mancini, *Pre-modernism*, 42, 94.
14. Harrod, *Real Thing*, 322.
15. "Teaching Boys to Make Good Furniture," 10.
16. "Making Box Furniture," 218.
17. For more on Karin Larsson, see Thorell, *Karin Bergöö Larsson*. A 1906 design by Karin Larsson was the basis for the Lillberg rocking chair sold by IKEA today (98).
18. Thompson, "Louise Brigham," 201. Brigham's correspondence with the Larssons is housed in the archives of the University of Uppsala, Sweden.
19. Many designers working in the Arts and Crafts and Art Nouveau styles liked to enclose type in squares and rectangles, but these were not often as strictly geometric and unornamented as Brigham's monogram.
20. For more on the design methods of Hoffmann and his students, see Houze, "Wiener Kunst."
21. Kardon, *Ideal Home*, 34, 40.
22. Kirkham, *Women Designers*, 97.

23. Louise Brigham, *Illustrated Lectures*, 15.
24. Thompson, "Louise Brigham," 199–200.
25. Brigham may also have been familiar with the geometric unit blocks designed by the New York-based educator Patty Smith Hill (1868–1946). In this connection, one similarly wonders if Brigham ever met Caroline Pratt (1867–1954), a sloyd-trained educator who was active in the New York settlement movement just after the turn of the century and who invented her own system of Froebel-derived geometric blocks, showing them at what was probably the same 1911 Child Welfare Exhibit that Brigham took part in. See Wellhousen and Kieff, *Block Play*, 10; Hauser, *Learning from Children*, 55–57.
26. Ovington, "Annual Report," 13–14.
27. "Miracles with Old Boxes." It is uncertain which precise span of years she is referring to, but something on the order of 1895–1908 is likely.
28. Gelber, *Hobbies* (212); Gillespie, "Women Who Count," 9. Crocker, in "Visit to 'Box Corner'" (775) says there were two Sunshine Cottages.
29. "Making Box Furniture," 218.
30. "Reviews," 595.
31. "Making Box Furniture," 218.
32. "Notes of the Week," 692.
33. Brigham, *Box Furniture*, 184.
34. "Notes of the Week," 692.
35. McClain and Long, "Aschermanns." In "How I Furnished" Part I (70), Brigham describes a brown and tan color scheme for the living room of Box Corner First.
36. "Miracles with Old Boxes," 3.
37. In the Preface to *Box Furniture* (4), Brigham lists the Elizabeth Peabody House—a Boston settlement house that still exists today although in a different location—as one place where her box furniture was either presented or installed, but it is unclear whether that happened before or after Brigham's years in Europe.
38. Throughout this book, numbers preceded by the pound sign (#) refer to the number of the design in Brigham's book *Box Furniture* (1909 edition).
39. See, for example, the careers of Octavia Hill in Great Britain or Jane Addams and Ellen Gates Starr in the United States.
40. Leavitt, *Catharine Beecher to Martha Stewart*, 77.

CHAPTER 3

Box Furniture

Abstract This chapter offers a close analysis of *Box Furniture*, the book Progressive Era designer and social activist Louise Brigham published in 1909 about making furniture from recycled packing crates. It offers an overview of several overlapping aspects of Brigham's book, including the aesthetics of box furniture, her foregrounding of multifunctional and modular design, and her commitment to a do-it-yourself approach to furniture making. Her aesthetic is analyzed in terms of how it reflects the values of contemporary design movements, especially Arts and Crafts and Josef Hoffmann's Wiener Werkstätte, and there is an examination of her work with the designer Edward H. Aschermann, who illustrated the book. Finally, there is a discussion of how the book fits into a burgeoning marketplace of advice writing and how box furniture aligned with the contemporary values of thrift and hygiene often promulgated by advice writers.

Keywords Louise Brigham · Box furniture · Edward H. Aschermann · Multifunctional furniture · Modular furniture · Advice writing

© The Author(s) 2019
A. LaFarge, *Louise Brigham and the Early History of Sustainable Furniture Design*,
https://doi.org/10.1007/978-3-030-32341-7_3

> To all who care for simplicity and thrift, utility and beauty, I send my message.
> —Louise Brigham, Introduction to *Box Furniture*, 1909

Somewhere along the way, while experimenting with box furniture at the Sunshine Cottage in Cleveland, on Spitsbergen, and in Copenhagen, Louise Brigham decided to publish a book about box furniture, likely with the encouragement of Hoffmann. Her book came out in 1909 under the deceptively plain title *Box Furniture: How to Make Useful Articles for the Home* (Fig. 3.1). It was published by the Century Company, a former subsidiary of Charles Scribner's and Sons that also published *Century Magazine* and *St. Nicholas Magazine*, a publication for children. *Box Furniture* is a small volume with a big set of goals. It is a do-it-yourself manual, a guide to thrifty living, a compendium of multifunctional and modular design, and an introduction to an aesthetic program.

Do-It-Yourself Manual

As a practical manual, its audience was the working poor. Every single item of furniture included—from the Plant-box (#1) to the Combination Reading Desk, Reading table, and Bookcase (#100)—is designed to be built out of ordinary wooden packing crates by modestly skilled householders. The individual pieces are shown in simple line drawings accompanied by detailed step-by-step instructions (Fig. 3.2). At the back of the book is a small selection of photographs of box furniture in use, along with a picture of Brigham's own tool-chest rather touchingly captioned: "The Tool-chest, given to the Author by One Hundred Friends."[1]

Interestingly, and quite unlike other writers of the day who published how-to articles on carpentry projects, Brigham did not provide detailed plans and cross-sections drawn to scale. In effect, she offered recipes rather than blueprints. This may have been in part a practical matter having to do with her materials. The packing crates on which Brigham's designs are predicated were made of rough pine, often with defects like knotholes. They were manufactured in all sorts of sizes and dimensions, from 4 × 8-inch bottle boxes to three-foot-long silk boxes. When Brigham's instructions called for a bottle box or a silk box, people would have known what she meant, but individual boxes were probably not made to very exacting specifications. It's possible that she felt that she could not safely specify her designs in quite the same detail as the typical article on home carpentry that called for the use of standardized lumber. More likely, she

Fig. 3.1 The cover of the first edition of Brigham's *Box Furniture*, 1909

> BOX FURNITURE 103 
>
> ### QUADRUPLE WRITING-DESK
> *Illustration 41*   *Figure 1*
>
> At this desk four persons may work, each having individual narrow and wide closets, with shelves for stationery and book compartments.
>
> **Requirements:**
>
> Bodies. 8 Soap Boxes (8 in. deep, 13¼ in. wide, 27¾ in. long).
>
> Shelves. 27 Pieces ½ in. thick, length and width equal to the inside width and depth of the box.
>
> Top. 1 Piece ¾ in. thick, 52 in. square (five boards wide).
>
> Tie Strips. 4 Strips ⅝ in. thick, 3 in. wide, 52 in. long.
>
> Corner Trim. 16 Strips ½ in. thick, 1¼ in. wide, length equal to the outside length of the box. 16 Strips ½ in. thick, 1¾ in. wide, length equal to the outside length of the box.
>
> Facing Strips. 8 Strips ½ in. thick, 1¾ in. wide, length equal to the outside length of the box.

Fig. 3.2 Design for Brigham's quadruple writing desk (#41), with storage units serving as the legs. Shown here is the first of three pages of instructions for building this desk (From her *Box Furniture*, 1909)

wanted to make it easier for someone to improvise by substituting one kind of box for another; she is careful in her instructions to give proportions of one element to another.

These kinds of crates were a relatively new development in the United States. Around the turn of the twentieth century, companies began shifting from selling loose goods to selling pre-packaged products.[2] Large corporations like Procter & Gamble began paying close attention to the design and standardization of the containers that were used to package their goods.[3] During this transition, many Americans burned packaging materials because they were still using wood stoves to heat their homes.[4] In one of her articles on box furniture, Brigham estimated that Americans burned over one million dollars worth of lumber each year in "ruthlessly discarded" boxes.[5] That is, in the early days of boxed goods, people generally saw the boxes as fuel rather than as something that could be upcycled in other ways. It wasn't until radiators and gas furnaces began to displace wood-burning stoves for heating and cooking that boxes became widely available for upcycling since they could no longer be used as home-heating fuel.[6]

Brigham had dedicated *Box Furniture* to the photographer-activist Jacob Riis, whose book *How the Other Half Live* influenced her "to lend a hand to the friendless," and to a childhood mentor, Cynthia P. Lane (possibly someone who helped to raise her after her mother died). Riis returned the compliment by praising her book effusively: "I had no idea that anything, at once so simple and so beautiful, could be made out of the cast-off boxes we burn so lightly, and yet I am myself a carpenter and love tinkering. I do think that you are performing a service not easily to be overestimated."[7] Similarly, other contemporary reviewers appreciated that Brigham was considering "from an economic standpoint" the "overlooked possibilities of waste material" that would otherwise be burned.[8]

Box Furniture opens with sound advice on how to choose the most useful of these crates and disassemble them without damaging the pieces. Brigham follows this with instruction in basic carpentry (how to clinch nails), and a short list of necessary tools. The designs call not just for simple and ubiquitous materials—canned-corn boxes, bottle boxes, soap boxes—but for simple construction techniques. Rabbeting—a method of cutting a notch or groove into the edge of a piece of wood—is probably the most demanding technique in the book and it is not introduced until three-quarters of the way through. Little is required to build any of the hundred pieces of furniture apart from a saw, hammer, brace (drill), measuring device, nails, and hinges. There are designs for everything from lanterns and stools to dressing tables and desks. There are a great many variations on the cupboard. At least two of the designs derive directly from the Spitsbergen summers: the Spitzbergen Sideboard (#89; see Fig. 1.3) and the Combination Reading Desk (#100; Fig. 3.3). Brigham writes that she was asked to construct this desk in such a way that its oil lamps could not be tipped over by the local cat "who has a fondness for lamps."[9]

Brigham organized her designs into suites for some fifteen different rooms, from kitchen, bedroom, and living room to studio, office, and library.[10] This "menu" or "tour" approach echoes a presentation format common to cookbooks and household books of the day.[11] Each room has

Fig. 3.3 One of Brigham's larger pieces of Spitsbergen furniture, 1906: a combination desk, reading table, and bookcase with built-in lamps, constructed from packing crates (rear view) (Photograph from her *Box Furniture*, 1909)

its own chapter, with the exception of the nursery—although the frontispiece is a drawing of a nursery, children's furniture is scattered throughout other chapters. Brigham further organizes the book so that more complicated pieces of furniture fall towards the end.

Each chapter has a design theme deriving from certain ways of handling the packing crates. For instance, in Chapter IV, the box "is taken partially apart so that it loses its original shape," whereas in Chapter X, the box is "taken partly or completely apart and the material used in construction." Design writer Larry Weinberg notes that this theme of disassembly foreshadows "the radical achievement of De Stijl architecture—the deconstruction of the box."[12] And as several authors have pointed out, the systematic nature of Brigham's process, from box disassembly to finished piece, marks a clear delineation between her project and more ad hoc proposals for repurposed packing materials.

Historian Katherine C. Grier has found scattered evidence of furniture made from packing crates and barrels in the second half of the nineteenth century.[13] For example, an 1878 book champions the use of packing crates to create small articles of furniture like washstands; while an 1885 article describes a home in the western United States furnished with box and barrel furniture covered in fabric.[14] The most common type overall seems to have been barrel furniture: mainly stools, chairs, and hampers, commonly with added padding or upholstery both for comfort and to disguise the furniture's lowly origins.[15] By the early twentieth century, a few companies had picked up on these ideas; they might suggest ways that their containers could be repurposed (for example, as lunch boxes), but these were public relations efforts rather than serious attempts at promoting recycling (or upcycling) as an ethos.[16]

Instructions for making this kind of furniture in the nineteenth century were often quite sketchy and assumed little in the way of carpentry skills. Some of this furniture may have been made by women living in circumstances where they could not count on male help with the carpentry and upholstery. Like Brigham's later crate furniture, these items were not made to be sold but were made by and for people who could not afford store-bought furniture. As they were not considered valuable objects, very few have survived into the present day.

Thrifty Living

Box Furniture appeared at a time when the average worker took home on the order of $4–$8 a week, and a single piece of factory-made furniture might cost a week's wages.[17] At that rate, it could take a long time to save for (or pay off) suites of furniture for every room. By contrast, Brigham showed that you could create an entire apartment's worth of box furniture for that same week's wages. Here and there she offers examples of particular designs in actual use somewhere: a small cabinet in an art studio, a game table in a settlement house—reassurances that the cheap materials needn't compromise the object's utility or longevity.[18] Curiously enough, *Box Furniture* itself, although priced in line with other clothbound books, was rather costly in light of its intended audience: it was advertised for sale at $1.60 plus 14 cents shipping—or roughly one-fifth to two-fifths of the average worker's weekly wage.[19]

As a guide to one aspect of thrifty living, *Box Furniture* belongs to what was by then the very well established field of domestic advice writing. In the United States, domestic advice writing extends back to the early nineteenth century with works such as Lydia Maria Child's *American Frugal Housewife* of 1828.[20] Later influential writers in this mode included Catharine Beecher (*Principles of Domestic Science as Applied to the Duties and Pleasures of Home*, 1870), Sarah Josepha Hale (*The New Household Receipt-Book*, 1854), and Julia McNair Wright (*The Complete Home*, 1878). In the 1870s and 1880s, another wave of advice books appeared that focused as much on interior decoration as on the practicalities of housekeeping. One well-known series, the "Art at Home" books, was published in both Britain and the United States between 1876 and 1883 and could well have formed part of Brigham's reading.[21]

Writers in this field tended to be middle-class women like Brigham, that is, women who had the education, the free time, the writing skills, and the connections necessary to make book publishing possible. They saw their job as assisting women of equal or lower social status whose knowledge was deficient, whether because they were young or because they lacked the opportunity to learn what was needed to run a household properly—a form of moral, aesthetic, and educational patronage that stemmed from nineteenth-century views of the mutual obligations of different social classes.[22] The later books also took increasing account of what became known as "the servant problem": the fact that as the landscape of job opportunities changed with advancing industrialization, fewer people (both men and women) went into domestic service and women had to adapt their housekeeping practices accordingly. The underlying assumption was that everyone aspired to a commonly understood better life, but that not everyone had the means to achieve those goals without careful management of what is now known as the "3 Rs": reduce, reuse, recycle.

These writers accepted the prevailing idea that the domestic sphere was the woman's responsibility and argued for thriftiness as both financially prudent and a sign of good moral character. By the end of the century, the moralizing approach infected all areas of domestic advice writing even as the writers' mandate expanded from the household to connected subjects such as sanitation, waste disposal, and public and private hygiene.[23] Moral values were attributed to homes and furnishings, so that it became important for furniture to be "honest" and well made, as an extension of the owner's character. The well-made became a stand-in for the good.

While their initial focus was on middle-class women like themselves, by the end of the century domestic advice writers had widened their scope to include the working class and new immigrants.[24] As this shift took place, domestic advice took its place as part of larger reform movements under way that targeted health and education as well as housing. Between 1900 and 1920—the period when Brigham was most active in promoting her box furniture and carpentry training workshops—the population of the United States expanded from 76 to 106 million, and about half of that increase was due to immigration.

The main form of thrift that *Box Furniture* advocates for is reduction of waste through recycling (though this term wouldn't come into use until the 1920s) and specifically upcycling. As one writer bluntly remarked, Brigham's book was "one of the few indications of the birth in this country of a tendency toward less wastefulness of raw material."[25] The noted Unitarian minister Jenkin Lloyd Jones expressed the most extreme version of this view when he wrote that her ability to create objects of utility and beauty out of "refuse" qualified her as an "eminent artist."[26]

In the nineteenth century, there was not yet any regular trash collection in most urban areas.[27] In addition, formal channels that accepted goods for recycling—charities like Goodwill and the Salvation Army—were not set up until the early twentieth century.[28] Households—and especially the women in those households—thus had to pay attention to salvaging and making-over worn-out objects in part because there was nowhere convenient to dispose of them. So it is not surprising that nineteenth-century advice books were full of recommendations for saving and reusing everything from string to clothing, tallow to ashes.

As Susan Strasser points out in *Waste and Want*, "nothing is inherently trash."[29] Something becomes trash when it is no longer wanted or needed, but also through carelessness or a need to demonstrate social power (that one can afford to waste goods).[30] And it becomes easier to consider something as waste when it can be put out of sight and out of mind. The notion that one might repair something rather than designate it as trash "comes more easily to people who make things,"[31] which was certainly the case with Brigham. It took a maker's mind—not to mention a bricoleur's confidence—for a young woman in the early twentieth century to consider that the thing she would do was to make furniture from scrap wood and then write a book about it. And as Strasser notes, remaking or making-over existing objects can call for even greater creativity than making something from scratch, because one must deal with the handiwork of the prior makers—their methods and choice of materials, their proportions and level of competence.[32]

Brigham was particularly early in her explicit advocacy of recycled *industrial* waste for furnishings.[33] The use of industrial castoffs didn't really take off until after World War II, in tandem with an invigorated critique of consumer culture and the wastefulness of mass production. Today, the use of recycled and other "green" materials focuses on two separate aspects: not wasting resources (so as to be able to meet future needs) and reducing the harms associated with industrialized materials (such as pollution).[34] In Brigham's era, as we have seen, most of the emphasis was on the former, but the idea of harm hovered in the background, implicated in the then-common view that associated wastefulness of any kind with sin (a moral harm). Specific aspects of today's sustainable design, such as the emphasis on energy efficiency, were not concerns in Brigham's day; but it is worth pointing out that her use of recycled industrial materials did have some built-in efficiency in that the packing-crate wood substituted for new lumber that would otherwise have had to be processed through the sawmills and shipped to the city to build her designs.

Brigham was also thoughtful in linking recycling to place, to identifiable local needs. This social practice probably stemmed from her training as a reformer, dealing with the problems of particular communities. There is nothing about her project that suggests a genuinely universalizing viewpoint: she was interested in helping New Yorkers of a specific class build the furniture they needed for their limited apartment spaces, and in training their children in basic woodworking skills. Furthermore, she did not merely demonstrate her techniques for others to adopt but also furnished several of her own apartments entirely with box furniture (see Chapter 4 for more about this element of her project). By living in these box furniture worlds, she valued the experience of place over things. In one sense, her apartments were sets for the public relations angle of her project, a point that will be developed further in Chapter 4.

Multifunctional and Modular Design

Box Furniture is also a guide to multifunctional, space-saving design and its first cousin, modular design. In Europe, multifunctional furniture traces back at least to the Middle Ages, with benches that had internal storage and chests that became beds or daybeds when closed; but if one looks beyond houses to consider the multifunctional features of long-distance ships, for example, one must clearly look for origins much further back in human history. By the nineteenth century, European and American furniture was being differentiated into specific uses: for example, multifunctional chests had separated into two pieces, a chest (usually with drawers) and a bed.[35] However, there was still a good deal of multifunctional furniture in use, such as fall-front desks and many variations on the wardrobe. New inventions escalated around the turn of the twentieth century as industrial ideals of rational planning and efficiency were transferred from the factory to the home.[36] The designer Gustav Stickley, for example, developed a compact wardrobe and published it in 1902 in his magazine *The Craftsman*, where Brigham's own work would later be featured.[37] To this day, a great deal of multipurpose furniture is only bi-functional, such as the ever-popular sofa bed, rather than complexly multifunctional.

In whatever era you find multipurpose and modular furniture, it signals that rooms themselves are understood as multifunctional rather than single-purpose: they can, for example, be living rooms by day, bedrooms by night; or dining rooms at mealtime and schoolrooms in between.[38] In small urban apartments, rooms often serve three or four uses: as living rooms, playrooms, offices, and bedrooms. Brigham's designs take into account the space constraints of urban apartment dwellers, who often need flexible-use and space-saving furniture such as drop-leaf tables and hidden cupboards. Moreover, her target audience of low-earning urban apartment dwellers could not afford the single-purpose rooms and furniture that allowed the middle class to move away from multifunctional and modular furniture for many decades. Brigham's multifunctional pieces include the quadruple writing desk with built-in bookshelves and storage units (#41), a corner seat for college students with built-in bookcases (#83), a combination washstand and wardrobe (#90), and several others. As this list suggests, one of the values her designs express is the importance of making space for books in modern life.

Brigham's designs are also strongly engaged with the potential of modularity—both in the aggregation of smaller units into larger pieces, and in the use of modular raw materials. The single most severely geometric piece of modular design in *Box Furniture* is the Nest of Benches for Kindergarten and Settlement (#67; Fig. 3.4). Despite its mundane name, it is almost the platonic ideal of the nested bench, a tightly fitted set of seven graduated shapes in unadorned wood. Brigham may have known about some of Josef Hoffmann's famously elegant designs for stacking tables by the time she came to write her book, but her own nesting benches were probably not influenced much (if at all) by Hoffmann as there is evidence that her design goes back to her work in the very early 1900s with a Cleveland settlement house. In this context, it may not be an accident that they evoke the sets of nesting blocks that had been popular children's toys since the late nineteenth century.[39] Stylistically, a closer cognate for Brigham's

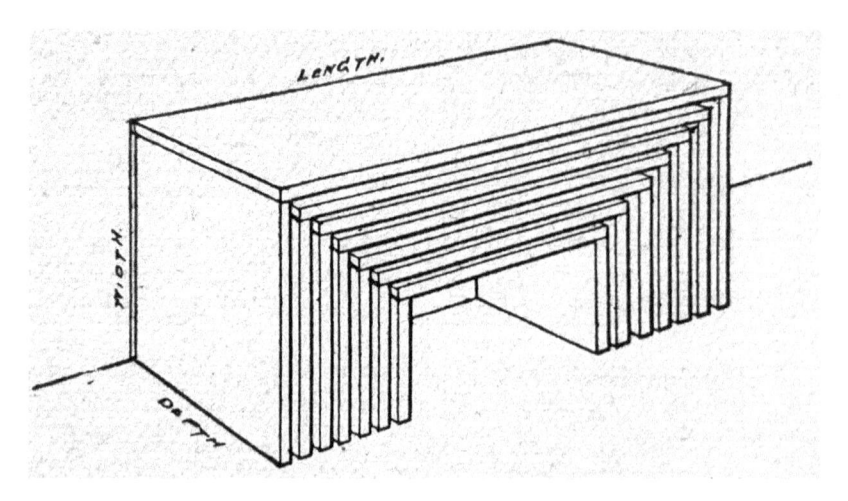

Fig. 3.4 Brigham's Nest of Benches from her *Box Furniture*, 1909

nesting benches are Bauhaus designer Josef Albers' nesting tables from the mid 1920s.

Brigham based many of her designs on the limited set of standard dimensions and shapes of common packing cases, which she then often broke down into repurposable pieces of pine sorted by size. Thus, the Small Wall Rack (#21), is constructed out of a condensed-milk crate with minimal recutting, yet it looks almost nothing like the original box. The Double Wall Rack (#28), is made by nailing together two #21s, while the Large Wall Book Rack (#29), consists of three #21s. The College Corner Seat (#83) is made by combining and slightly modifying two #53 Flower and Book Stands and a #81 Window seat.

As these examples indicate, some of Brigham's pieces are simple enough that they could readily be placed side by side to create a larger, unified look such as one achieves today with IKEA-style matching units. As the writer Larry Weinberg notes, one of the few precursors to Brigham's pioneering work in this respect is the famous Globe Wernicke unit bookcase. In the mid-1880s, the American furniture manufacturer Wernicke Company of Grand Rapids, Michigan, invented a set of glass cabinet units of varying sizes that could be stacked in different ways to create what it called "elastic" bookshelves (Fig. 3.5). This modular shelving design was patented in 1892, and a few years later the company merged with another to become Globe Wernicke. When the patent expired around 1912, this kind of unit-based modular design began to expand, though it wouldn't really take off in the United States until the 1930s, when Donald Deskey and Gilbert Rohde designed a line of sectional furniture that is often taken as the starting point of modern modular furniture design.

Brigham falls chronologically in the middle of the time span between Globe Wernicke and Deskey and Rohde. Her system emerged during the period when Globe Wernicke still dominated the world market for this type of furniture, and it is quite possible she was familiar with their system, which was especially popular with lawyers and other white-collar professionals.

Aesthetic Program

Box Furniture is not only a practical handbook; it is an introduction to an aesthetic program. Brigham constantly refers to the "beauty" of her designs, and she intends no irony. People of small means have probably been making furniture out of castoffs since earliest history; Brigham is

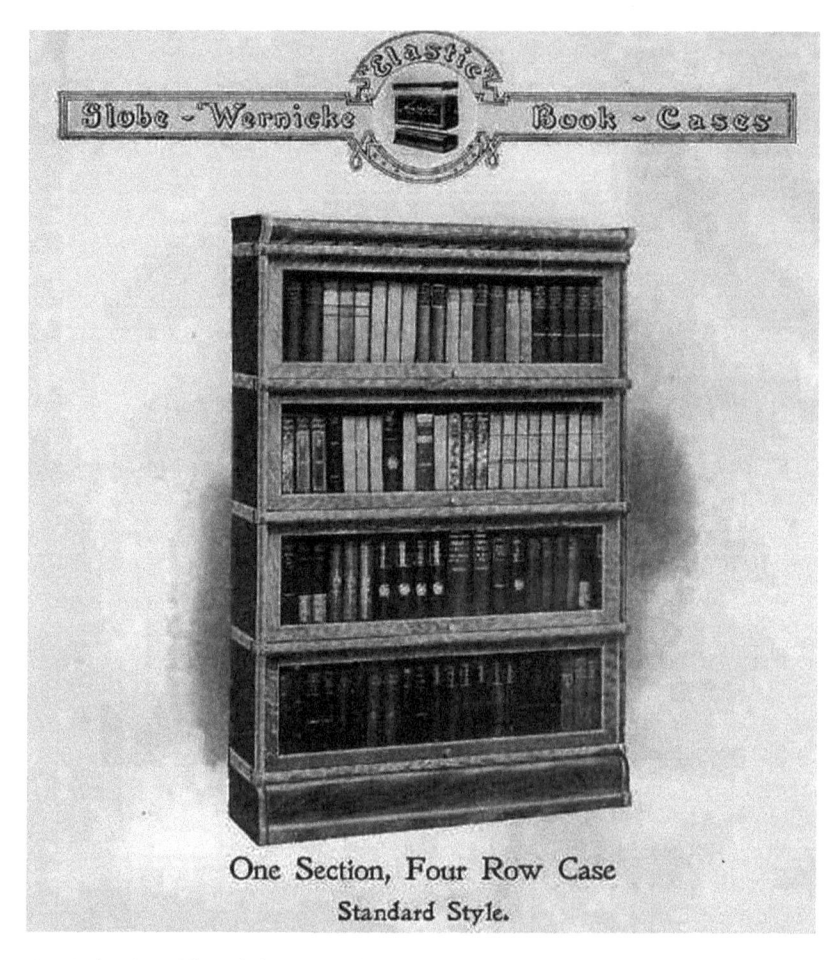

Fig. 3.5 An ad for Globe Wernicke's "elastic" bookcases (Photo from Wikimedia Commons)

seeking to handle this same kind of material with respect and without aesthetic compromise. Brigham mentions John Ruskin and William Morris—the progenitors of the Arts and Crafts movement—as inspirations,[40] and although she doesn't discuss this at any length, there are clear affinities with the Arts and Crafts valuation of individual handicraft and a turn away from mass production. In the United States, the Arts and Crafts style flourished between the mid-1890s and World War I and its proponents were often aligned with the Progressive movement. Brigham would likely have become aware of it through many channels, including art school and her work in the settlement movement, as the American Arts and Crafts Society was founded in a Chicago settlement house. Morris and Ruskin were also influences on Hoffmann's interest in craftsmanship and folk arts.

But when it comes to form, Brigham turns away from the flowing lines and intricate nature-inspired motifs of Arts and Crafts objects and explicitly aligns her "severe, geometric"[41] aesthetic with that of Hoffmann, with his focus on the square as a fundamental unit of design. Early in the book, writing about the use of decoration to complement box furniture, she says: "The simple motifs shown in the several interiors are an adaptation of the 'Hoffmann method' of utilizing the square as the basic principle in decoration.... This method makes it possible to have attractive rooms decorated in a simple manner without any special art training."[42]

Brigham's designs also show a distant stylistic kinship with the then-mature Prairie School and Mission styles of furniture associated with Frank Lloyd Wright, Gustav Stickley, and others. In addition, box furniture has strong affinities with American rustic furniture of the day, much of which was developed for the summer homes, cabins, and camps of the middle class.[43] A good example of this is the Adirondack chair, designed by Thomas Lee in 1903. Yet Brigham makes no claims to align with any of these movements.[44] All of them depended in one way or another on the rectangle as a key form, but it would be hard to overstate how much plainer and more uncompromisingly rectilinear Brigham's "beautifully basic designs"[45] are than the furniture made by any of the above-mentioned designers. All but the very plainest rustic furniture tends to incorporate curves, lathe-turned elements, and subtle ornamental details that Brigham avoids.

Even when refined through sanding, paint, and the addition of cushions, her pieces retain a starkness that won't come into its own until after World War I. The finishes she recommends are commercial paints (especially white), dark stains, and varnishes, but there is none of the obsession with high finish that was common among furniture makers of the day.[46] Yet there is plenty of evidence that she is looking at other artists for inspiration: a table with an unusual (for Brigham) octagon-shaped top, or a flag wall rack directly inspired by an encounter in Scandinavia with the hobby of collecting national flags.

The chief aesthetic appeal of Brigham's box furniture lies in its early modernist appreciation for lightly ornamented rectilinear forms that are kept subservient to the functional requirements of daily life. Weinberg points out that Brigham's designs can appear both clumsy and derivative of the Mission style,[47] but I would argue that this is largely an artifact of her atypical commitment to low-value material, semi-skilled construction, and plain finishes. Mission furniture was often made of hardwoods like oak that finished well, and although it was intended to appear handmade, it was often partly manufactured in factories, with minor curvilinear elements to soften its form.[48]

There are also subtler aspects of Brigham's aesthetic that speak to her close engagement with her materials. Packing-crate wood was often a thinnish, low-quality pine that was further compromised by nail holes, knotholes, and manufacturing defects. To strengthen box furniture, many of Brigham's designs call for plain finishing strips of corner and edge trim. These reinforcements also function as visual framing, lightly emphasizing each piece as a composition in rectangles.[49] In some pieces (see, for example, Fig. 3.3), they also create regularly spaced vertical emphases that evoke the vernacular verticality of Carpenter Gothic board-and-batten work and some of Gustav Stickley's slatted chairs.

Brigham commissioned the book's line drawings from the interior designer Edward H. Aschermann, who was one of a handful of avant-garde American designers whose work was infused with the sensibility of the Vienna Secession and Wiener Werkstätte in the first decade of the twentieth century.[50] The son of German immigrants, Aschermann, like his near-contemporary Brigham, had trained in Europe, where one of his mentors was Josef Hoffmann.[51] He met Brigham through Hoffmann, and they became lifelong friends who shared a holistic approach to design, an appreciation of the handmade, and an ethos of frugality.[52] In later years she would visit Aschermann and his wife and design partner, Gladys Aschermann, at their Maine summer home, River Rocks.[53]

Aschermann's style aligned with that of other leading draftsmen and illustrators of the day like the architect Harvey Ellis (who frequently contributed drawings to *The Craftsman* magazine) and the printer William Joseph "Dard" Hunter, who was heavily influenced by Josef Hoffmann and worked at the famous Roycroft Press in New York.[54] All of them favored a strongly linear graphic style with limited detail, an emphasis on shapes, and washes or patches of flat color.

Aschermann's freehand construction drawings in *Box Furniture* appear somewhat informal, and it is likely that Brigham gravitated towards this aesthetic—instead of, for example, the precision of technical drawings— for a lessened intimidation factor. Yet her avoidance of highly polished drawings may also contribute to an overall impression of amateurishness that can extend to the designs themselves, causing them to be devalued by some readers.[55]

In addition to drawings of individual pieces of furniture, Aschermann created half a dozen views of complete rooms (Fig. 3.6). These are intended to show how box furniture can be part of an overall design scheme that echoes the furniture's geometrical styling in wall stencils, curtains, and other design elements. As McClain and Long write of these views: "The square—and a multitude of variations on it—governs the geometry of the furniture and the configuration of the whole."[56]

Aschermann's room views are carefully constructed bits of representational theater: The individual pieces of furniture look light (though not fragile), and the rooms themselves spacious and open—much less cluttered

Fig. 3.6 Edward H. Aschermann's drawing of a dining room scheme for Brigham's *Box Furniture*, 1909

than the book's photographs of actual box-furnished rooms. His drawing of the dining room, for example, is framed like a stage, with the spectator looking into it from the fourth wall. No doors awkwardly interrupt any of the three visible walls: it is a pure idea of a room.[57] Photographs of the box-furnished dining room in Brigham's own apartment make the room seem cramped and crowded in comparison to Aschermann's expansive drawings, with individual pieces appearing heavy and slightly oversize in the small space.

Aschermann's drawings are accompanied by detailed color treatments for every element of the room, right down to the choice of plants. For example, the den is to be painted in two shades of buff with deep red furniture, accented by cream curtains, jute rugs, and natural linen pillows with mahogany motifs. This modern take on a Colonial-era palette is brightened through the choice of yellow, orange, or red flowers. A black, white, and crimson color scheme is recommended for the living room, where black-painted furniture and woodwork stand out from white walls with crimson wall hangings.[58] Brigham will later employ this color scheme in one of her own box-furnished apartments.

At the turn of the twentieth century, Americans were used to mainly white and muted-color rooms; the use of bold colors to express a modernist sensibility moved in slowly over a couple of decades.[59] For example, Hazel Adler's *The New Interior: Modern Decorations for the Modern Home* of 1916 was one of the earlier books advocating for strong color schemes.[60] Indeed, both Aschermanns would shortly become known for their sophisticated use of color as an element of interior design—they were capable, for example, of juxtaposing a living room done in orange, light gray, and black, with a violet hall leading to a dining room done in canary yellow, blue, and black.[61] McClain and Long consequently argue that the color schemes of *Box Furniture* probably owe more to their aesthetic than to Brigham's. Few of Brigham's writings or interviews suggest that she was deeply concerned with color; her first interest always lay with the furniture itself and the specific social conditions within which it was intended to exist.

Another important aspect of Brigham's design program was her interest in reducing clutter, both physical and visual, through the use of multifunctional furniture and through avoidance of ornamentation. Starting in the early twentieth century, domestic advice writers and interior designers began to inveigh against the fussily furnished home as symbolized by the Victorian parlor (Fig. 3.7). Their arguments followed two separate lines of thought, one based on hygiene and efficiency and one on aesthetics.

Fig. 3.7 An Edwardian living room, as published in *Ladies' Home Journal*, November 1, 1910, in an article immediately following Part III of Brigham's "How I Furnished My Entire Flat with Boxes"

The Progressive Era saw the rise of a hygiene movement as part of a larger interest in public health. Clutter came to be seen as unsanitary—all that "dust-catching, insect-breeding, microbe-sheltering"[62] array of plush furniture, heavy drapes, and large rugs. At around the same time, an increasing value was placed on efficiency in all spheres, extending outward from the studies of industrial workflow carried out by researchers such as Frederick Taylor and Frank Gilbreth Sr. For instance, the Taylorist home economist Christine Frederick wrote extensively about ways to improve household efficiency, especially in the kitchen; Brigham could well have come across her articles in *Ladies' Home Journal*, for which Frederick served as an editor.[63] The fact that clutter was inefficient as well as unsanitary loomed as an ever-larger problem when women started moving into the workforce and demanding ways to spend less time on housework.

At the same time, modernists were dismissing Victorian interiors—typified as overfurnished and old-fashioned—on aesthetic grounds. The modernist argument against this "tyranny of things" (as Smith called it)[64] also positioned decoration as a form of visual clutter; modernism was associated with the removal of all nonessential, nonutilitarian elements.[65] As Smith wrote, the typical person with a Victorian aesthetic thought that "the more machine scroll work, gorgon heads and claws, the more big brass handles, the more stuffing, the more colors in the plush, the better."[66] The modernist ideal was to "cultivate the beauty of harmony and simplicity," avoiding such aesthetic horrors as a "whatnot full of useless trash."[67] There was a strongly gendered aspect to this argument: Victorian decoration was decried as feminine and modern simplicity was praised as masculine by the male artists and critics who were modernism's most vocal proponents.[68] Proto-modernist women like Brigham were placed in an awkward position: in trying to escape the bounds of domesticity imposed on women in the nineteenth century, they found themselves involved in a discourse that continued to privilege men and to associate avant-garde ideas with masculinity.

An influential event in the turn toward modernist interiors came with a 1902 exhibition at the Mechanics' Fair in Boston, where a Victorian living room was explicitly and unfavorably contrasted with the new modernist designs featuring simplicity and minimal furniture.[69] But it required more than a decade for the modernist aesthetic to take full root. Writing about Mabel Hyde Kittredge's model flat in 1905, Bertha Smith observes that "simplicity is not yet the creed of the many"[70] and that some of Kittredge's modernist innovations—such as dispensing with all rugs in favor of bare floors—were looked on askance.

Some advice writers tried another tack to interest modernism-averse readers, pointing to other cultures as models; ideas drawn from Japanese and Native American cultures were especially favored in this period.[71] Brigham herself wrote an illustrated article for the *Ladies' Home Journal* in 1910 with detailed instructions on how to make baskets and rugs from "products of Nature's garden" like corn husks, rushes, grasses, pine needles, willow withies, and fern stems.[72] Here Brigham's interest in reuse of materials intersects neatly with her love of crafts and folk art. Her emphasis was on items that "cost nothing," and she barely mentions any of the cultures in which such crafts are traditional—there is a single passing mention of the Pocumtuc, a Native American tribe from Massachusetts. Nor does she give much information on where an *LHJ* reader might procure the raw materials, or how to prepare them for use in weaving. "Gather the rush in August, and use when well seasoned" is an instruction that leaves out a great many important points such as location, species, size, and timing, to name just a few of the more obvious ones.[73] In writing for the *LHJ* readership, she seems to have understood that she was addressing an audience of traditional hobbyists. Elsewhere, as we shall see, she more clearly imbricated certain handicrafts with a modernist aesthetic.

Brigham's book appeared toward the end of a period in which publications on art and interior decoration had expanded enormously in scope and influence. These magazines helped to solidify the idea that women were responsible for "producing" domestic interiors, a task that Brigham took up in an unusually holistic way.[74] In Chapter 4, we will see her operating with a new hat, that of the interior designer, as she builds out her own apartments, overseeing everything from the furniture to the wall treatments to the textiles and metalware.

Notes

1. Brigham, *Box Furniture*, 298.
2. Strasser, *Waste and Want*, 113.
3. Strasser, *Waste and Want*, 14.
4. Strasser, *Waste and Want*, 113, 137.
5. Louise Brigham, "How Boys Make Furniture," 242.
6. Strasser, *Waste and Want*, 173. In her book *Box Furniture*, Brigham includes a design for a bookcase framed to fit an apartment fireplace no longer in use due to steam heating.
7. Brigham, *Illustrated Lectures*, 16.
8. Dille, "Miss Louise Brigham," 6; Crocker, "Visit to 'Box Corner'," 779.
9. Brigham, *Box Furniture*, 289. It sounds as if Brigham may be quoting here from a letter, which suggests the possibility that William Munroe was in touch with her about building some furniture even before she arrived on Spitsbergen.
10. The bathroom is the major exception. The closest she comes is with plans for washstands in the office, bedroom, and dining room, no doubt reflecting the realities of life for the working poor. There is also an "invalid's bed-table" with a lower compartment for "night conveniences" (i.e. a chamber pot). *Box Furniture*, 99, 171, 207, 252, 255, 265, 269.
11. Leavitt, *Catharine Beecher to Martha Stewart*, 49.
12. Weinberg, "Thinking Outside the Box."
13. Grier, *Culture and Comfort*, 274; Strasser, *Waste and Want*, 28, 64.
14. Strasser, *Waste and Want*, 65–66.
15. Gelber, *Hobbies*, xx; Leavitt, *Catharine Beecher to Martha Stewart*, 93; and Strasser, *Waste and Want*, 20.
16. Strasser, *Waste and Want*, 172. Additionally, a few manufacturers around the turn of the century were making barrel chairs as part of the Colonial

Revival (66). Barrel furniture seems to be a hardy perennial, because in the early twenty-first century, tables made from whiskey barrels were being sold on Amazon.
17. The average annual income in the United States in 1910 was on the order of $200–$400 (slightly higher in the Northeast). See Klein, "Personal Income" and Gelber, *Hobbies*, 213. Similar figures for Great Britain can be found in Edwards, "Furnishing a Home," 233–239.
18. Brigham, *Box Furniture*, 97, 146.
19. Century Co. advertisement, date uncertain, probably Summer 1911.
20. Leavitt, *Catharine Beecher to Martha Stewart*, 9–10.
21. For more on nineteenth century advice writing on interior decoration, see Aynsley, *Design and the Modern Magazine*; Aynsley and Berry, "Publishing the Modern Home"; and Ferry, "Any Lady Can Do This."
22. Leavitt, *Catharine Beecher to Martha Stewart*, 83. For more on the subject of patronage and social class, see Harrod, *Real Thing*; Helland, "Good Work and Clever Design."
23. Leavitt, *Catharine Beecher to Martha Stewart*, 37–48.
24. Leavitt, *Catharine Beecher to Martha Stewart*, 75; Smith, "Gospel of Simplicity," 84.
25. "Book of Boxes."
26. Brigham, *Illustrated Lectures*, 16. The fact that Lloyd Jones was Frank Lloyd Wright's uncle raises the question of whether Brigham was more connected to the Wright circle than writings by and about her suggest. However close or distant the connection, it is certainly the case that the Reverend Jones's approval in no way implies that Wright would have felt the same way.
27. Strasser, *Waste and Want*, 23.
28. Strasser, *Waste and Want*, 140.
29. Strasser, *Waste and Want*, 5.
30. Strasser, *Waste and Want*, 9–10.
31. Strasser, *Waste and Want*, 10.
32. Strasser, *Waste and Want*, 10.
33. In fine art, the use of recycled materials is often placed as originating with Pablo Picasso's early twentieth-century invention of collage; but a wider view that included the applied arts would have to take into account other starting points, such as the histories of the quilt or decoupage. In any case, I am only arguing for Brigham's early use of such materials in the field of interior design, not art construed more broadly.
34. Williams, *Sustainable Design*, xxiv.
35. Edwards, "Multum in Parvo," 17–18.
36. For more on multifunctional furniture, see Edwards, "Multum in Parvo"; Showalter and Driesbach, *Wooton Patent Desks*; and Hiller, *Hoosier Cabinet*.
37. Edwards, "Multum in Parvo," 20.
38. Ferry, "Any Lady Can Do This," 154.

39. The popular Crandall's Nesting Blocks, for example, were patented in 1881. See Provenzo and Brett, *Complete Block Book*, 16–18.
40. Brigham, *Box Furniture*, Preface, 2.
41. Kirkham, *Women Designers*, 98.
42. Brigham, *Box Furniture*, 6.
43. The term "rustic furniture" also includes pieces made of logs and twigs, which don't overlap with Brigham's project at all.
44. Gelber (*Hobbies*, 213) points out that Brigham's designs "were clearly at home in the age of Stickley."
45. Attfield, "What Does History Have to Do with It?"
46. On the question of finishes, see, for example, Kardon, *Ideal Home*, 48.
47. Weinberg, "Thinking Outside the Box."
48. Kardon, *Ideal Home*, 69.
49. "Making Box Furniture," 219.
50. Thompson ("Louise Brigham," 201) notes that in Brigham's correspondence with the Swedish painter Carl Larsson, she at one point discussed having him illustrate a book for her. It's unclear why this never happened, or even whether it would have been a different book altogether.
51. McClain and Long, "Aschermanns." Due to anti-German sentiment around the time of World War I, the family anglicized their name to 'Asherman,' but to avoid confusion I will use the original spelling throughout this book. According to McClain (personal communication), a family friend of the Aschermanns thought that Aschermann and Brigham had studied together at the Wiener Werkstätte, but this has not been independently corroborated.
52. McClain and Long, "Aschermanns."
53. McClain, personal communication. Apparently Brigham was known as 'Aunt Louise' to the Aschermann family.
54. One of Hunter's best-known designs is a rose stylized to fit within a square, which became a signature image of the Arts and Crafts movement. Similarly, Brigham designed her own monogram to fit within a square.
55. A later (c. 1915) edition of *Box Furniture* includes an illustration by a different (uncredited) artist. It is a vignette of a room featuring Brigham's #76 Greek-cross Tea table in the middle ground with an armchair in the foreground. With its fussy detailing, it contrasts strongly with Aschermann's work and makes Brigham's furniture seem banal and rather rustic, something one would find in a seaside cottage rather than an urban apartment. (See Adkisson, "Box Furniture: Thinking Outside the Box," 10, for a reproduction of this image.) It is unclear why Brigham would have chosen to proceed with such a radical shift of illustration style and tone in the later edition.
56. McClain and Long, "Aschermanns."
57. There are also between one and three windows, though the drawing is ambiguous enough that these may instead be pictures or shallow shelving units. These eye-level renderings of furnished rooms are similar to some of

Harvey Ellis's compositions, though Ellis generally uses washes more liberally than Aschermann.
58. Only a few years later, black-and-white room decoration schemes were so much in vogue that they became targets for satirists. See "Black and White Vogue," 45.
59. Leavitt, *Catharine Beecher to Martha Stewart*, 138.
60. Leavitt, *Catharine Beecher to Martha Stewart*, 137.
61. Aschermann and Aschermann, "'Modern' Interior Decoration," 81.
62. Smith, "Gospel of Simplicity," 83.
63. See, for example, Frederick, *The New Housekeeping*.
64. Smith, "Gospel of Simplicity," 84.
65. Leavitt, *Catharine Beecher to Martha Stewart*, 79, 105; Smith, "Gospel of Simplicity," 83.
66. Smith, "Gospel of Simplicity," 85.
67. Priestman, *Art and Economy*, 18, 188–189.
68. Leavitt, *Catharine Beecher to Martha Stewart*, 99–104.
69. Leavitt, *Catharine Beecher to Martha Stewart*, 79, 98.
70. Smith, "Gospel of Simplicity," 86.
71. Leavitt, *Catharine Beecher to Martha Stewart*, 149–155.
72. Brigham, "Rugs and Baskets," 31.
73. Brigham, "Rugs and Baskets," 31.
74. For more on women as producers of designed interiors, see Aynsley and Berry, "Publishing the Modern Home."

CHAPTER 4

The Social Program

Abstract This chapter turns to the social program underlying the box furniture of Progressive Era designer and social activist Louise Brigham, focusing on the several channels through which Brigham publicized and advocated for box furniture apart from her 1909 book *Box Furniture*. In addition to writing magazine articles (especially for Ladies' *Home Journal*) and giving talks, Brigham made a practice of furnishing her own New York apartments with box furniture and turning them into public showplaces for the aesthetic and social value of her project. Her holistic approach to the interior design of these apartments extended beyond her box furniture to items like linens that she herself designed and made, as well as wall treatments. Following a brief consideration of Brigham's work with the New York-based Home Industries' Association, the chapter surveys the industrial expositions at which Brigham showed entire rooms of box furniture, placing both these exhibits and the showcase apartments as variants of the "model homes" that were a common feature of Progressive Era social projects.

Keywords Louise Brigham · Box furniture · Model home · Box Corner First · *Ladies' Home Journal* · Women's Industrial Exposition · Panama-Pacific International Exposition · Home Industries' Association

© The Author(s) 2019
A. LaFarge, *Louise Brigham and the Early History of Sustainable Furniture Design*,
https://doi.org/10.1007/978-3-030-32341-7_4

Fig. 4.1 Drawing of Brigham's dining room furnished with box furniture, from the third installment of Brigham's article "How I Furnished My Entire Flat with Boxes" in *Ladies' Home Journal*, November 1, 1910 (Uncredited drawing, possibly by George A. Newman)

Brigham was a tireless champion of her book and her box furniture system during the years before and during World War I. She gave numerous newspaper interviews and wrote articles in popular magazines—indeed, I first stumbled on her work in a 1910 issue of *Ladies' Home Journal* in which she published one installment of a four-part article entitled "How I Furnished My Entire Flat from Boxes."[1] The accompanying illustrations of box furniture (Fig. 4.1) leaped out at me by the strong contrast they posed to the surrounding articles and advertisements promoting the highly finished, padded, tasseled, embroidered, and lace-accented furnishings that conventional taste then demanded. Steven Gelber argues that practically none of the middle-class women who made up the *Ladies' Home Journal* audience would have wanted to make Brigham's furniture for themselves.[2]

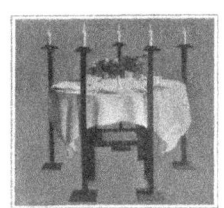

Fig. 4.2 Several possible configurations of the Greek-cross table both with and without its matching floor-based candlesticks, as published in *Ladies' Home Journal*, March 1910 (Image courtesy of HathiTrust, https://hdl.handle.net/2027/mdp.39015011414193)

This might be true on aesthetic grounds, but it is noteworthy that Brigham gives much more detailed and technical instructions for how to build her box furniture than would be needed for a simple overview or puff piece. Although the main purpose of this article was to publicize Brigham's project among people who might help to further it in other ways, it is not incidental that one could actually build the furniture by following Brigham's directions.

This article was one of many that Brigham wrote for *Ladies' Home Journal* focusing on aspects of box furniture or on general handicrafts. Some of the others focused on narrower topics. One item was a page of captioned photographs of furniture for children, including pieces that weren't in her book, such as a rocking cradle and a rideable "Rocking Rabbit."[3] Another discussed the many ways her eye-catching Greek-cross-shaped table (#76) could be used. By raising and lowering its four hinged leaves, it was possible to change the table's configuration in several different ways (Fig. 4.2).[4] Brigham also described a very unusual matching set of nearly 4-foot-tall, free-standing "portable" wooden candlesticks that looked particularly dramatic when set into the angles of the table in its Greek-cross configuration.[5]

Brigham made a point of living with box furniture, pragmatically turning a series of apartments into showcases for her project, to which she brought a constant stream of visitors. Here she collapses the distinction sociologist Erving Goffman drew between the public spaces of social performance and the private "offstage" space of the house; in Brigham's apartments, her private arrangements were deliberately organized in order to facilitate a public performance of box furniture and herself as its intermediary.[6]

Fig. 4.3 A drawing (possibly after a photograph) of the four sides of the living room at Box Corner First by George A. Newman, as published in *Ladies' Home Journal*, September 1, 1910 (Image courtesy of HathiTrust, https://hdl.handle.net/2027/mdp.39015011414193)

The *Ladies' Home Journal* observed, "No one has, perhaps, ever attempted the actual and complete furnishing of an entire suite … from the most ordinary grocery store boxes."[7] Over a span of some months, Brigham furnished her five-room apartment at 589 E. 89th St. on the corner of East End Avenue almost entirely with box furniture made from her own designs and customized to the apartment's small rooms and architectural idiosyncrasies. All told this took 55 boxes, most of them free but a few that cost as much as 15 cents apiece, for a total cost of $4.20 (roughly the equivalent of $108 in 2019).[8] It became known throughout this working-class neighborhood as the House with the Window Boxes since it featured a set of window boxes made from cocoa boxes and "swung on balancing cords in the Japanese fashion."[9] She named it Box Corner First, a name as stripped down as her furniture. It would have several successors.

Some of the illustrations and dark-printed photographs in Brigham's book can give a misleading impression of crudeness in the finished objects. The illustrations accompanying her four-part article in *Ladies' Home Journal*, some of which were drawn by the painter George A. Newman,[10] give a better idea of the quality of Brigham's designs and their aggregate effect (Fig. 4.3). For the living room at Box Corner First, she designed a bookcase with double doors that looks like a direct ancestor of IKEA bookcases (Fig. 4.4), but the most ingenious piece is undoubtedly her elaborate writing desk (Fig. 4.5). This desk has a portfolio case for drawings built into the back, as well as extra drawers and shelves and a small file cabinet on top. There is even a specially designed recess for an inkpot.

From Baked-Beans Boxes

Fig. 4.4 Brigham design for bookcase with double doors, as published in *Ladies' Home Journal*, September 1, 1910 (Image courtesy of HathiTrust, https://hdl.handle.net/2027/mdp.39015011414193)

The desk is attached to a tall cabinet made in three sections, one of which is a bookcase and the other two of which have been designed to accommodate sets of commercially available file cases.[11] The unusual combination of elements—especially the portfolio case—suggests a piece designed to accommodate Brigham's own needs and desires, making it one of the most personal designs in her entire oeuvre.

Brigham used her favorite blue-and-white color scheme in the bedroom of Box Corner First, and she chose a gray-and-white scheme with crimson

Fig. 4.5 Brigham design for a combination writing desk (with portfolio case) and file cabinet, as published in *Ladies' Home Journal*, September 1, 1910. This design is not included in Brigham's *Box Furniture* (Image courtesy of HathiTrust, https://hdl.handle.net/2027/mdp.39015011414193)

accents for the kitchen on the grounds that gray "is the color of dust, and with a coal stove in use freedom from dust is quite impossible."[12] Around the top of the kitchen walls, she lettered a chain of domestic mottoes such as "A Good Cook Means Much Tasting and No Wasting."[13] There was even a motto in German over the entry door to the kitchen: "Willkommen zu dem Heim der Fräulein Brigham" (Welcome to Miss Brigham's home). This neatly combines a performance of domestic production of "the home" with a performance of design authorship.

The dining room was dominated by her Greek-cross tea table, and all of the furniture and woodwork in the dining room of Box Corner First was stained an unusual gray-green. Brigham even found a cheap patterned wallpaper that was a similar color on its back side and used it, wrong side out, to cover the walls.[14] It is evident from her description of this room that the room's secondary colors came mainly from the metal dishware and silverware.[15]

Like some of today's designers, Brigham accented her rooms with handicrafts, many of them picked up on her travels: for instance, a Hungarian shepherd's crook, Breton pottery, British doorknobs of hammered metal.[16] Her appreciation of folk art links her to other European avant-garde designers of the day, such as the Hungarian-American Ilonka Karasz, as well as to artists who participated in the folk art revival that swept across Eurasia in the early twentieth century as part of the search for national identity, from Ireland and Scandinavia to Russia and beyond. In Russia, it was closely allied with modernism, and a number of modern artists like Kasimir Malevich and Natalia Goncharova designed clothing and textiles using folk motifs or worked with regional craftspeople.[17] Art critics were not enthusiastic about the crafts-based work by avant-garde artists like Malevich; in effect, the aura of craft trumped the avant-garde elements and made the work seem less impressive than his very similar work in painting.

Brigham also made a number of items for her own apartment. She wove the living room's blue-bordered linen curtains and couch covers herself and enameled a set of coffee spoons.[18] She stuffed the cushions of a window seat with wood shavings left over from the construction process.[19] These touches are a reminder of the ordinary expectations for a middle-class home of the period (enameled coffee spoons!) and at the same time of the personal investment that sets Brigham's and the Aschermanns' do-it-yourself approach apart from most such homes. As she put it: "In order to have the work recognized as a power for good my home must be beautiful as well as practical."[20] And the cushions, which turn up in many of Brigham's seating designs, signal both an appreciation for comfort and an understanding that the basic geometries of box furniture did not necessarily conduce to that comfort on their own. Here we see an essential difference in Brigham's approach from that of "pure" designers like Frank Lloyd Wright, some of whose Prairie furniture was famous for being hard to sit on for very long. It was important to her that box furniture be as easy as possible to live with.

In the final installment of "How I Furnished My Entire Flat from Boxes," Brigham reports that she had had over 500 visitors at Box Corner First in the prior 18 months. Articles on her apartments that were written up for a number of publications can be seen as early versions of the then-emergent genre of the celebrity home essay.[21] One reporter was quite openly surprised at the quality of the furnishings in Brigham's flat: "People are not in the habit of looking at a substantial, well made combination desk and bookcase…and recognizing off-hand the packing boxes seen languishing in the basement last week."[22]

Anticipating this reaction, Brigham had cannily left original crate labels in place on hidden parts of the furniture to confirm their origins and thus "assist the hard taxed credulity of the visitor." Other adjectives used by this reporter in describing the box furniture include "beautiful" and "ingenious." Another writer stated flatly: "There is nothing crude in box furniture."[23] It is something of a tribute to Brigham's skill in both making and talking up her work that she was able to elicit such positive reactions. Around the same time that Brigham was furnishing her first flat with box furniture, Edward Aschermann turned his own apartment into a showcase of similarly modern design that he subsequently had to tone down because it was too radical for "conservative American tastes."[24] There is a suggestion here that if the well-to-do of North America weren't quite ready for modern design for themselves, they didn't mind championing it for those less well off. What couldn't yet pass as high design was acceptable as thrift.

Some visitors argued that the charm of Box Corner First owed more to the folk art and craftwork add-ons than to Brigham's own unusual furniture, and Brigham responded to this implicit challenge two years later by furnishing a second apartment in the same building, where she owned four units altogether.[25] Box Corner Second (Fig. 4.6) was a more explicit homage to Brigham's Viennese mentor Josef Hoffmann in its austere black-and-white color scheme accented by a few touches of brilliant color. One of the armchairs in Box Corner Second looks like a simplified variant of Gustav Stickley's Morris chair in which the side slats have been replaced, in typical Brigham fashion, by a built-in magazine holder.[26] Brigham installed her chief assistant in Box Corner Second.[27]

Sometime later, Brigham set up Box Corner Third, still in the same building. This five-room apartment housed no less than 63 items of box furniture, many of the pieces multifunctional in ways that shipbuilders or today's micro-apartment dwellers would appreciate. The Week-End Cabinet, for example, appears to be a bookcase until you open a side door, revealing a small closet; while the top opens out into a dressing table and mirror (Fig. 4.7). Neither this cabinet nor the divan to which it is attached featured in Brigham's book, underlining the fact that her ingenuity did not stop with those first hundred designs.[28]

Brigham also gave talks about her work in the United States and abroad using magic-lantern slides (a method of projecting images).[29] Around 1914, she published a small illustrated pamphlet, probably as publicity material for these lectures.[30] *Illustrated Lectures* consists mainly of captioned photographs of box furniture in different settings, accompanied by praise of Brigham's work quoted from various sources. There was an address to which one could write for details on lecture terms and dates. This pamphlet represents the single best collection of photographs of Brigham's furniture in use.

Fig. 4.6 The living room at Box Corner Second, as published in Brigham's *Illustrated Lectures*, ca. 1914. Designs for the large armchair at left and the combination table-bookcase at center are not included in Brigham's *Box Furniture*. The pair of smaller chairs could be Brigham's Desk Chair (#40) with padding (Photo courtesy of the Museum of the City of New York)

Brigham's systematic and holistic approach to furniture design has obvious links to the furnishing programs of contemporaries like Frank Lloyd Wright and Charles Rennie Mackintosh, but it is clearly differentiated from those highly publicized oeuvres by the fact that Brigham was not chasing a luxury market, and the fact that she ultimately focuses on a social rather than a primarily aesthetic program. Weinberg calls it "a comprehensive system attached to a design theory and a social agenda." And it was this aspect of her work that ultimately drew the most attention and praise.

Although the socially utilitarian aspects of box furniture reflect Brigham's years in the American settlement movement, she did not (so far as is known) continue her work with the settlement movement after she published *Box Furniture*, instead turning her reformist ideas about education and design in other directions entirely. As her own furnished apartments demonstrate, she was acutely aware that three-dimensional models

Fig. 4.7 The box furniture corner seat at Box Corner Third, as shown in *Illustrated Lectures*, ca. 1914. At the right-hand end is the multifunctional Week-End Cabinet. This design is not included in Brigham's *Box Furniture* (Photo courtesy of the Museum of the City of New York)

were more persuasive than the two dimensions of drawing or photography.[31] So she also created scale models and public exhibits as a way of reaching a broad public of social reformers, newspaper writers, educators, and other people of influence.

One of these exhibits was "Room Delightful," an entire suite of box furniture for a child's room that Brigham installed at a Child Welfare Exhibit that traveled from New York City (1911) to Chicago (1911), Buffalo (1912), and Rochester (1913).[32] Created out of 54 boxes, it consisted of 17 articles of furniture suitable for a boy of 12, a girl of 9, and a baby (Fig. 4.8). Among these were a high chair, a combination double desk and bookcase (an elegant design that does not appear in Brigham's book), a music stand, and a number of tables and chairs. The entire collection, displayed in a three-sided temporary room, cost $10.47 to make.[33]

Fig. 4.8 A model room of box furniture at a Child Welfare Exhibit, New York, 1911, as published in *Illustrated Lectures*, ca. 1914 (Photo courtesy of the Museum of the City of New York)

Similarly, in the early spring of 1912 and again in 1913, New York hosted a Women's Industrial Exposition at the Grand Central Palace showcasing the achievements of women "for improvement in both work and play" in such areas as hygienic production of milk, organization of children's "day nurseries," sewing, and cooking.[34] Brigham took part in 1912 by lending the suite of bedroom furniture from Box Corner First, and in 1913 by lending living room and nursery furniture (Fig. 4.9).[35] Two years later, at the enormous 1915 Panama-Pacific International Exposition in San Francisco's Palace of Education and Social Economy, Brigham set up a large exhibit in the Palace of Education featuring seven box-furnished rooms taken from her own homes.[36] She also box-furnished a Montessori School with a suite in blue, gray, and white, an effort that won her a medal.[37] She also apparently ran a box furniture-making workshop at this exposition.[38]

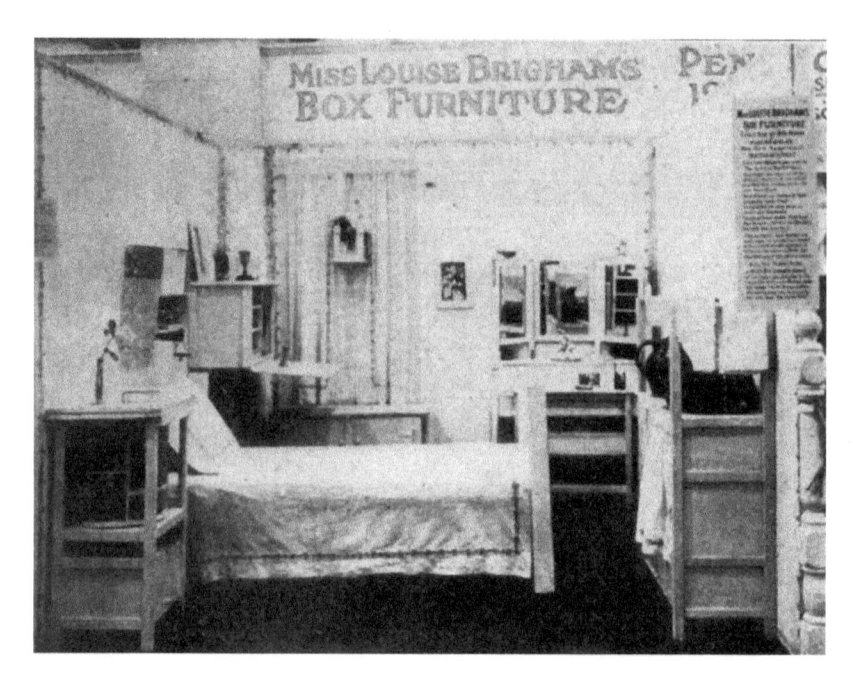

Fig. 4.9 A model room of box furniture at the Women's Industrial Exposition, Grand Central Palace, New York, 1912, as published in Brigham's *Illustrated Lectures*, ca. 1914 (Photo courtesy of the Museum of the City of New York)

Similarly, in 1910 she organized the inaugural exhibit of the Home Industries' Association (HIA) on E. 34th St. in New York, which featured handicrafts by European and American women—lace, basketry, embroidered textiles, and pottery alongside box furniture.[39] Like the similarly named Home Arts and Industries Association (HAIA) in Great Britain, the HIA was founded to encourage home-based trades, especially those focused on skills traditionally associated with women.[40] The HAIA had been very active and well-publicized in the 1880s, holding exhibitions and running classes to teach various craft skills (including woodworking), and it is quite possible that Brigham knew about it and took it as a model for the HIA as well as for carpentry workshops she began teaching in 1911 (see Chapter 5 for more on these workshops).

Like the settlement house movement, the HIA was part of a large constellation of women-led homosocial voluntary organizations intended to engage women's lives with the public sphere.[41] In the interview Brigham gave the *New York Times* when this show opened, one sees clearly her protofeminist championship of women in the workforce and her hostility to the industrial sweat-shop side of modernism inflected through a middle-class patronage model of social progress:

> We want our American women to rouse themselves to the patronage of handmade work instead of the cheap machine-made stuff that is sold in the cheaper shops.... We are having Europe's humble class coming to our shores by the thousands. Almost without exception the woman has her own little diversion in the shape of knitting, or lacemaking, or something of the sort. Should we not encourage those women in their home industries and thus make better citizens of them?[42]

Brigham's apartments—and to a lesser extent her installations at industrial expositions—can be seen as variants of the "model homes" that were a frequent element of social projects of the day.[43] To help immigrants integrate into American ways of living, domestic advice writers, home economists, social workers, and social reformers set up model homes, often using them as sites for teaching classes. Model homes featured as part of the settlement house movement with which Brigham had been affiliated early in her career; for example, the Henry Street settlement in New York had a tenement apartment set up as a model home.[44] While some of these were semi-permanent, similar but temporary home demonstration setups like the ones Brigham created would appear at festivals, fairs, and expositions.

The idea for using model houses originated no later than the 1890s and continued well into the twentieth century. An early example appeared at the World's Columbian Exposition in 1893, where the social reformer Katharine Bement Davis was the director of the New York State Workingman's Model Home. She fitted out the model house with furniture, utensils, and even a model family.[45] A decade later, the home economist Mabel Hyde Kittredge set up the first of a series of model four-room tenement flats and "housekeeping centers" in New York. The idea was to demonstrate how a home could be furnished nicely on a budget of $500, with chairs, for example, costing no more than $5.[46] It seems likely that Brigham was directly inspired by Kittredge's work when she turned her own apartments into model flats demonstrating the virtues of modernist design generally and box furniture specifically. However, it is instructive that Kittredge's limit of $500 is two orders of magnitude higher than the $4–$10 range Brigham spent for entire rooms or apartments worth of box furniture.

Few of these model homes were as personal as the apartments Brigham furnished and lived in. Indeed, it's quite possible that Brigham was seen as an eccentric for living in those box-furnished apartments with their Japanese-inspired window boxes. Seen in this light, an example that is close to Brigham in spirit is Gwenthean Cottage in Boulder, Colorado, a model home built by domestic scientist Theodosia Ammons.[47] She and her sisters each spent time at the cottage, and Ammons gave classes there every summer as part of the Texas-Colorado Chautauqua summer school, which was mainly attended by teachers. The cottage still exists with many of its original furnishings.[48] There is an innate theatricality to the model home—an intersection of private space and public spectacle—and nowhere is this more visible than when the model is lived in, as with Gwenthean Cottage and Brigham's apartments. In Box Corners First through Third, Brigham was performing her version of domesticity in the public spotlight.

Brigham's project as a whole aligns with a Vicwardian ideal of middle- and upper-class women as social reform leaders. Victorian Britain saw the rise of women sponsors of all kinds of "social architecture," ranging from schools and colleges to workers' housing, hospitals, and clubs.[49] The United States similarly benefited from the social leadership of such women, and Brigham's setups at the expositions of 1911–1913 can certainly be understood as this kind of social architecture. The demonstrations she set up at industrial fairs and expositions were designed to transfer knowledge mostly within, rather than across, class. Primarily, they represented her activities to potential patrons of her project.

Some of the American reformers also saw themselves as preservers of threatened cultural traditions such as Native American arts or the crafts that European immigrants brought to their new country. In order to preserve and circulate knowledge about crafts, such reformers promoted demonstrations that could serve as educational devices to transfer knowledge of these craft activities to middle-class consumers—an approach that has been referred to as "paternalistic pastoral."[50] Brigham's deployment of European crafts in her apartments and her 1910 article about basket-weaving all played this kind of role. Most of Brigham's project, however, focused on knowledge transfer in another direction, toward the working class. Her book was one outgrowth of this effort, but another highly visible example is the Home Thrift Association, an organization she founded primarily to run carpentry workshops for working-class children.

NOTES

1. Brigham, "How I Furnished." The four installments were published once a month from September to December 1910. The first article focused on the living room, while subsequent installments focused successively on the bedroom, dining room, and kitchen.
2. Gelber, *Hobbies*, 213.
3. Brigham, "Made for the Child," 43.
4. Louise Brigham, "One Table," 39. Brigham designed two false tops, one round and one a large square, to further increase the ways in which the table could be used.
5. The candlesticks are not included among the plans in *Box Furniture*, but Brigham writes about them in "One Table." They were weighted with lead to increase their stability.
6. See Goffman, *Presentation of Self*.
7. Brigham, "How I Furnished," Part III (Editorial Note), 80.
8. Brigham, "How I Furnished," Part I, 70. The exceptions were a few pieces she had made herself or brought home from her European travels. See "Teaching Boys to Make Good Furniture," 10, and Gelber, *Hobbies*, 213. Note that the size of the apartment is uncertain: Gelber describes it as having four rooms rather than five, as does *Ladies' Home Journal*. There may be a confusion here between Box Corners First and Third.
9. "Miracles with Old Boxes," 3. Also "Making Box Furniture," 219. Contemporary writers referred to Brigham's neighborhood as a "slum" (Dille, "Miss Louise Brigham") and a "tenement" neighborhood ("Miracles with Old Boxes").
10. On stylistic grounds, this was probably George A. Newman (1875–1965), a realist painter and occasional illustrator from Pennsylvania. He also supplied a pair of bedroom drawings for Part II of "How I Furnished," and the drawings for the remaining two parts may also be by him, but uncredited, as the style is very similar.
11. Brigham, "How I Furnished," Part I, 70, 74.
12. Brigham, "How I Furnished," Part II, 86 and Part IV, 68; also "Miracles with Old Boxes," 3. She also chose gray because it would match a readily available line of inexpensive agateware (marbled stoneware).
13. Brigham, "How I Furnished," Part IV, 68.
14. Brigham, "How I Furnished," Part III, 80.
15. Apparently, Brigham got in the habit of preferring metal dishware during her residence in Sunshine Cottage, where the presence of children ensured a good deal of breakage. See "Making Box Furniture," 218.
16. Brigham, "How I Furnished," 80; "Teaching Boys to Make Good Furniture," 10. Brigham also placed art on the walls, and here her tastes ran to the conventional rather than the modern— Madonna-and-child paintings are an evident favorite.

17. Alfoldy, *Neocraft*, 195–201; Parker, *Subversive Stitch*, 193.
18. "Teaching Boys to Make Good Furniture," 10. A different source states that the curtains were unbleached cotton rather than linen.
19. "Making Box Furniture," 219.
20. Brigham, "How I Furnished," Part IV, 68.
21. Aynsley and Berry, "Publishing the Modern Home."
22. "Miracle with Old Boxes," 3.
23. Crocker, "Visit to 'Box Corner'," 779.
24. McClain and Long, "Aschermanns."
25. Dille, "Women Who Lead the Way," 6; also Brigham, *Illustrated Lectures*.
26. Brigham, *Illustrated Lectures*, 9.
27. This unnamed assistant may well have been Miss Ethel Bret Harte, referred to in Brigham's *Illustrated Lectures* in what appears to be the role of agent or assistant. The writer Bret Harte had a daughter named Ethel, and the unusual full name makes it likely that this was the same person. Born in New Jersey in 1875, Bret Harte's daughter would have been an exact contemporary of Brigham (Scharnhorst, *Bret Harte*, 114). She lived in England from 1898 until the early 1900s, returning to the United States sometime after 1905 (Scharnhorst, *Bret Harte*, 215, 232).
28. Even on Bermuda, where Brigham went for vacations—for example, in the summer of 1914, as Europe was heading for war—she furnished a small cabin from boxes and named it Box Nest. Brigham renovated this cabin as well, adding a veranda that ran around at least two sides and enlarging an end window. Built as it was out of sawn blocks of coral—a fairly common construction material on Bermuda—Brigham's cabin on Bailey's Bay may still exist today. Brigham, *Illustrated Lectures*, 14.
29. In Howes, *American Women* (vol. III, 164), she is listed as lecturing on box furniture in the United States, the Orient, and the Near East.
30. Brigham, *Illustrated Lectures*, ca. 1914. The approximate date of publication can be deduced from internal evidence; especially the statement that when the pamphlet went to press, Brigham was working on an exhibit for the upcoming 1915 Panama-Pacific International Exposition in San Francisco.
31. Pigza, "Rescuing Cast Offs."
32. Pigza, "Rescuing Cast Offs"; Brigham, *Illustrated Lectures*, 4.
33. Crocker, "A Visit to 'Box Corner'," 775; Brigham, *Illustrated Lectures*, 4. That the desk was a double one is inferred from the symmetrical design and from two photos published in these sources, each showing a child working at a different side of the desk. Interestingly, a nearly identical photograph, with slightly different furniture and featuring a woman working at the desk in place of the children, was tagged as "Miss Brigham's office" when published with the 1911 article "Making Box Furniture" in *The Craftsman*.
34. "Planning the Women's Industrial Exposition," 2. The 1913 exposition ran February 27–March 8.

35. Brigham, *Illustrated Lectures*, 16.
36. "Money and Art Happily Mated," 16.
37. "Glass Classroom"; Thompson, "Louise Brigham," 204.
38. Leavitt, *Catharine Beecher to Martha Stewart*, 92–93.
39. "Exhibition to Aid Home Industries," 10. The HIA received scanty press coverage and may not have survived very long.
40. For more on the HAIA, see Helland, "Good Work and Clever Design."
41. Kardon, *Ideal Home*, 34.
42. "Exhibition to Aid Home Industries," 10.
43. She may also have been inspired by some of Hoffmann's students, especially the group known as *Wiener Kunst im Hause* (Viennese Art at Home), which designed and displayed fully furnished rooms at various exhibitions. See Houze, "*Wiener Kunst*."
44. Leavitt, *Catharine Beecher to Martha Stewart*, 80.
45. Leavitt, *Catharine Beecher to Martha Stewart*, 80.
46. Smith, "Gospel of Simplicity," 83–86; Leavitt, *Catharine Beecher to Martha Stewart*, 80.
47. "Gwenthean" is a portmanteau word combining Ammons' first name with those of two sisters.
48. Leavitt, *Catharine Beecher to Martha Stewart*, 84–85.
49. Attfield, "What Does History Have to Do with It?," 9.
50. Adamson, *Thinking Through Craft*, 112.

CHAPTER 5

The Home Thrift Association

Abstract This chapter describes efforts by the Progressive Era designer and social activist Louise Brigham to train working-class children in carpentry through an organization she founded in New York City, the Home Thrift Association. Launched in the then-disused Gracie Mansion, the HTA migrated around the city over the several decades of its existence. The HTA apprentices produced box furniture for their own homes as well as for Brigham's showcase apartments. In its ethos and goals, the HTA was aligned with skills-training organizations like the Home Arts and Industries Association in Great Britain that emerged under the influence of ideas promulgated by William Morris and John Ruskin. In founding the HTA, Brigham also almost certainly drew on the ideas of John Dewey and the tenets of the Scandinavian sloyd movement, with which Brigham had become familiar during her European travels.

Keywords Louise Brigham · Box furniture · Home Thrift Association · Sloyd · Gracie Mansion · John Dewey

© The Author(s) 2019
A. LaFarge, *Louise Brigham and the Early History of Sustainable Furniture Design*,
https://doi.org/10.1007/978-3-030-32341-7_5

> Experimenting surpasses studying. Invention, and reinvention too, is the essence of all creative work.[1]
>
> —Josef Albers

The success of the 1911 Child Welfare Exhibit prompted New York City officials to offer Brigham space in Gracie Mansion in Carl Schurz Park for further experimentation. (At the time, Gracie Mansion had been shut up for years; it would not become the New York mayor's residence for another three decades.) Brigham accepted the offer and in that same year established a woodworking "laboratory" where boys would learn basic carpentry skills.

The workshop was open to girls as well, but ironically (given Brigham's own skills) they were not taught carpentry—that would happen later, and in a different context. Instead, they practiced more traditional girls' skills, making items in support of the boys' projects, such as mattresses and tablecloths.[2] In the early twentieth century, reformers and advice-givers generally believed that innate differences between girls and boys meant that they should receive different kinds of training for adult life.[3] Despite her own background and career, Brigham did not entirely escape this way of thinking; girls as a group get very little attention during her years of work with box furniture apart from a few articles that she wrote for *Ladies' Home Journal*.[4]

Brigham thought that it was pointless to attempt anything "with the small, useless tools which are often found in a child's cheap tool-chest."[5] So each boy would be given a basic set of good-quality tools—a crosscut saw, ripsaw, hammer, screwdriver, hand drill, plane, square, vise screw, and ruler.[6] With these, he would then make his own toolbox, as well as a workbench and vise, according to an ingenious method Brigham had worked out some years earlier in Norway.[7]

The boys themselves collected most of the packing crates that would provide their raw material, although Brigham would also apparently pay local tradesmen small fees to save better-quality boxes for her.[8] Some historians have concluded that such street scavenging was an almost universal activity of working-class children.[9] Most of the time they would sell the collected waste to various kinds of junk dealers (if they weren't taking it home to burn for heat). In this case, the boys would take the crates to the Gracie Mansion workshop, where they would disassemble them and sort the resulting lumber by length (Fig. 5.1).[10]

In order to support the workshop and all of the boys' toolkits, Brigham founded the Home Thrift Association, with one James B. Clemens as its first

Fig. 5.1 HTA boy with lumber from dismantled packing crates, sorted by size. From "Making Box Furniture" in *The Craftsman*, November 1911 (Image courtesy of HathiTrust, http://hdl.handle.net/2027/gri.ark:/13960/t17m7c85n)

president.[11] The HTA aimed "not only at thrift, but at the conservation of the home."[12] The boys—"apprentices" in HTA lingo—were encouraged to take home to their families the furniture they made in the shop, and they often did so, especially items for their young siblings such as cribs and small chairs (Fig. 5.2). Some of these apprentices—at their own request[13]— made most of the furniture for Brigham's various showcase apartments. "It is great fun when [the boys] come here to see me," wrote Brigham. "They know who made every bit of furniture. So do I. They feel, which is just what I want them to feel, that my house is a part of the community, and the community life."[14]

Despite the fact that she herself had drawn up plans for all kinds of furniture, Brigham encouraged the boys to be inventive and was pleased that no two articles ever came out quite the same.[15] She even reported that they sometimes made Morris chairs (probably modeled on Gustav Stickley's popular 1904 version) rather than furniture from her own designs.[16] In a more lighthearted vein, the boys made toys for themselves out of leftover scraps of wood: dump trucks and trolley cars, freight trains and derricks, a watermill and a lighthouse; even a small sail wagon for land yachting around the streets of New York.[17] Here Brigham is encouraging not only the essence of do-it-yourself culture, which merges producers

Fig. 5.2 Home Thrift Association boys taking home completed furniture (Photo courtesy of the Museum of the City of New York)

and consumers back into a single person, but also the added value of self-expression, which helps to turn ordinary objects into personal artifacts.[18]

The HTA workshop was open after school, in the evenings, and on weekends. Brigham did not require any kind of formal enrollment for the HTA; the boys could just show up whenever they felt like it.[19] With dozens of apprentices working in the shop after school, it was seen as a way to reduce juvenile delinquency. As Weinberg observed, "Brigham's educational platform…speaks more to vocational training than art education; it is more about keeping boys (and girls) off the streets than about cultivating a generation of designers or design conscious citizens." Brigham herself put it this way: "Two things help to make good results in box furniture—good boxes and good boys—although I have found the results from the combination of good boxes and bad boys to be equally successful, simply because, in my experience, I have found 'bad boys' to be 'good boys'."[20]

The Home Thrift Association took off, growing from 115 to 600 apprentices in its first year of operation.[21] This proved to be too many boys for Brigham to teach and organize alone, and she took on as an assistant the businessman and communitarian reformer Ralph Albertson, who had volunteered to help out after seeing her box furniture at the 1911 Child Welfare Exhibit.[22] Squeezed at first into just a couple of rooms in Gracie Mansion, it quickly expanded to six rooms.[23] An early exhibition of the boys' work in the workshop itself helped to promote the HTA.[24] Within a year, the need for more space prompted a move to what became known as the Home Thrift House at 516 E. 89th Street, just down the street from Box Corner First.[25] Brigham continued to work with the Home Thrift Association for several decades,[26] and there are indications that the idea of the Home Thrift Association spread to other parts of the country as well. Apparently, Father Edward J. Flanagan, who ran the Boys Town orphanage in Nebraska, set his boys to producing box furniture to be sold around the country.[27] In a 1935 issue of *Practical Home Economics*, home economist Altha Tedrow wrote about teaching Native American girls at the Pipestone Indian School in Minnesota to make furniture from recycled boxes.[28] The furniture she described included a chest, a baby bed, a dressing table, and a clothes closet. This article is notable for the number of different pieces of furniture it covers; apart from Brigham's work, earlier articles that touch on making furniture out of boxes typically only describe a single item of furniture (usually a chair or stool). It suggests that Tedrow might have come across and been inspired by Brigham's book.

Through the Home Thrift Association, Brigham made yet another kind of connection back to her Svalbard summers. Once, on a camping trip to Yosemite, someone asked her if it would be possible to make more comfortable camp furniture.[29] Brigham responded to this in her own way, designing a collection of camping gear whose umbrella title—Tak-Apart Furniture—suggests that she ultimately focused more on portability and collapsibility than comfort, and that she may (for once) have had an eye to commercializing an aspect of the box furniture project. A photograph of some HTA boys using Tak-Apart Furniture on holiday shows them sitting on nestable storage boxes under a wooden canopy with laddered legs—a very distant cousin of the "portable house" Brigham had furnished on Spitsbergen a decade earlier (Fig. 5.3).

For Brigham, all the different elements she taught the HTA boys—making and learning tools, collecting wood, building useful articles, creating their own designs—were critical to her program. She felt that training given to children in carpentry and other manual skills often failed because there was too much reliance on what she termed "externals": "If the pupils could

Fig. 5.3 HTA boys camping with Tak-Apart Furniture. From Brigham's *Illustrated Lectures*, ca. 1914. Original photo credited to Brown Brothers (Photo courtesy of the Museum of the City of New York)

be encouraged to [work] with materials found in the home, they would find near at hand a practical opportunity for creative activity."[30] As this remark shows, the Gracie Mansion laboratory was in part an expression of what has been called "masculine domesticity," an infusion of what were seen as male interests and skills—such as carpentry—within the domestic sphere.[31] And it was also an expression of some of the leading educational ideas of its day, especially those of the American philosopher John Dewey and the Scandinavian sloyd movement.

Dewey thought the foundation of education was not rote learning but knowledge gained through experience, by which he meant direct experience with objects and processes. His emphasis on practical experimentation opened the door to bringing training in craft skills into the schools. Manual training was seen as a way to develop the ability to think abstractly and to acquire skills that might be useful for any number of professions. It also taught the value of labor: it was a kind of hands-on civics lesson with a socialist tinge.[32] While Dewey's influence really took off after World War II, one of his most influential books, *The School and Society*, was published in 1899 and may well have inspired Brigham, who obviously shared his belief in the value of hands-on experience with tools.

A parallel strain of thinking emerged from the sloyd movement, which arrived in the United States in the late nineteenth century. Sloyd is a term for several closely related systems of handicraft-based education that originated in Scandinavia, notably Finland and Sweden. The word stems back to an old Teutonic root meaning to "strike" or "make"; as an adjective, sloyd means "handy" or "deft" and as a noun it means something close to the word "craft."[33] During the first half of the nineteenth century, the word sloyd was applied chiefly to the making of useful objects for daily peasant life. With increasing industrialization, however, traditional sloyd activities began to disappear, and a number of educators began thinking about how to bring them back. Over time, sloyd became a descriptor for various educational programs that placed training in handicrafts at their center.

In Sweden, sloyd as a system was refined and popularized by the educator Otto Salomon, who set up one of the early schools in the 1870s. Sloyd training expanded to the United States in the mid-1880s, when Lars Erikson set up a short-lived sloyd school in Minneapolis. After that school failed, Erikson went to Boston, where he taught at the Sloyd Teacher Training School on North Bennet St., which was founded in 1888 by Gustav Larsson. Another early sloyd promoter in the United States was the Finnish-born educator Meri Toppelius, who set up sloyd classes in the Chicago public school system.

Brigham became familiar with sloyd during her European travels, when she studied at the Sloyd Institute in Naas. She may also have had contact with some of the American sloyd schools, especially the one in Boston, where she grew up. Brigham's belief in handicraft as a path to social betterment, her focus on practical objects, her attention to the linkage between the workshop and the home—all of this is straight out of the sloyd philosophy. A progression from simpler to more complex tasks is another sloyd principle that Brigham made use of in several ways: it is visible in the organization of her book as well as in her method of having her apprentices begin by making their own workbench and toolbox.

A remark from one of Brigham's articles about box furniture sums up her approach to the HTA and how she determined to make use of her European experiences: "When I came home [from Europe] and talked about box furniture and other crafts, people said how very interesting it all was, and how unfortunate that those things couldn't be done in America. Of course, I made up my mind to show people that 'those things' could 'be done in America'."[34] "Those things" refers not only to the teaching of craft skills along the lines of sloyd or the Home Arts and Industries Association in Great Britain but also to the communitarian ethos of the HTA. An important feature of Brigham's approach to the HTA is that she is not placing more labor at the service of classes that are already oversupplied in that commodity. By encouraging her trainees to take their furniture home, she directed both the labor and the products of that labor back to the benefit of the working class itself. Her workshops and designs became a "power tool for the disenfranchised,"[35] a way to get a foot in the door of social mobility and creative freedom. The HTA thus stands in a long history of American informal education, from the lyceum movement and Chautauqua schools that flourished in the nineteenth century right through to today's makerspaces and do-it-yourself movement.

Notes

1. Adamson, *Thinking Through Craft*, 84.
2. "Making Box Furniture," 221.
3. Leavitt, *Catharine Beecher to Martha Stewart*, 132.
4. See, for example, "If a Girl Wants a New Curtain," 75.
5. Brigham, "Furniture from Boxes," 241.
6. "Making Box Furniture," 220.
7. Brigham, "Furniture from Boxes," 244. Given the mention of Norway, it's possible that Brigham got the idea for this from someone associated with the sloyd movement.
8. Brigham, "Furniture from Boxes," 242.
9. Strasser, *Waste and Want*, 115 (citing David Nasaw).
10. Brigham, "Furniture from Boxes," 241–244.
11. This was probably the James B. Clemens who was a New York physician and neighbor of steel tycoon Henry Frick. See Dille, "Women Who Lead the Way", 6; "Teaching Boys," 10.
12. "Teaching Boys," 10.
13. "Teaching Boys," 10.
14. "Teaching Boys," 10.
15. Brigham, "Furniture from Boxes," 342.
16. Brigham, "Furniture from Boxes," 342.
17. Brigham, "Furniture from Boxes," 440–444. Land sailing had only just emerged as a sport in Europe in the preceding decade. Following Brigham's

article is a short piece on "sailing on wheels," which was apparently so new a sport in the New York of 1915 that the writers weren't yet sure what to call it. For more on the HTA toys, see also "Making Box Furniture," 220; Dille, "Women Who Lead the Way."
18. For more on these aspects of DIY culture, see Edwards, "Home Is Where the Art Is."
19. "Teaching Boys," 10.
20. Brigham, "Furniture from Boxes," 241.
21. Gelber, *Hobbies*, 213; "Teaching Boys," 10.
22. Kallman, "Pilgrimage of Ralph Albertson," 385–386.
23. Dille, "Women Who Lead the Way" (10) gives 3 rooms as the inaugural number and 6 as the expansion.
24. Brigham, "Furniture from Boxes," 342.
25. The philanthropist Emily Vanderbilt Sloane, who would later serve as a president of the HTA, helped to fund-raise for this move. (Kallman, "Pilgrimage," 385). The HTA moved again, in 1937, to 350 E. 88th St. In "Making Box Furniture" (221), there is a statement to the effect that New York Parks Commissioner Charles Bunstein Stover acquired some of the HTA's production as a "permanent exhibit", but this seems to have long since disappeared. Stover served as Parks Commissioner from 1910 to 1913.
26. In 1940 she was honored by the HTA board for having worked with the association for more than a quarter century. See "Six Women Honored," 8.
27. Personal communication from Sidney Kirkpatrick. This would have been in the 1920s or later, suggesting a lingering influence for Brigham's project.
28. Leavitt, *From Catharine Beecher to Martha Stewart*, 92. Cardboard boxes are mentioned explicitly, as are wooden orange crates. Interestingly, Leavitt refers to Louise Brigham as an "anthropologist and explorer" rather than a designer or inventor. It is worth noting that the Pipestone Indian School was one of the Indian Residential Schools set up to assimilate Native American children to European culture, often under extremely coercive conditions. The context in which Tedrow was teaching girls to make recycled furniture is thus different from that in which Brigham was working a generation earlier.
29. Brigham, *Illustrated Lectures*, 13.
30. Brigham, *Box Furniture*, Preface, 3.
31. Kardon, *Ideal Home*, 32.
32. Adamson, *Thinking Through Craft*, 78–81.
33. For more on sloyd, see Eyestone, "Influence of Swedish Sloyd," 28–29; Clover and Hrenko, "Crafting Bridges Between Cultures," 256; and Larsson, *Sloyd*, 15–18.
34. "Teaching Boys," 10. For a later example of Brigham in the same vein, see also "Exhibition to Aid Home Industries," 10.
35. MacDonald, *"The Value of 'Sloppy Craft',"* 124.

CHAPTER 6

Ready-to-Assemble Furniture

Abstract This chapter examines several attempts by the Progressive Era designer and social activist Louise Brigham to commercialize her box furniture system. Around 1915 she founded the Home Art Masters company to manufacture and sell her I-Ma-Da line of ready-to-assemble (RTA) flat-pack furniture kits, an effort that was several decades ahead of the first really successful ventures into RTA furniture. In addition, toward the end of World War I she opened a school to train young women in carpentry, with an associated store where their products (especially toys) could be sold.

Keywords Louise Brigham · Box furniture · I-Ma-Da furniture · Ready-to-assemble furniture

Within five years, *Box Furniture* had gone through several editions and had been translated into a number of foreign languages (including Danish). It was widely reviewed and praised, and the influential magazine *The Craftsman* (founded and edited by Gustav Stickley) ran a long, admiring article on it in 1911.[1] In addition, Brigham suffered that least welcome form of praise, plagiarism. As historian Steven Gelber dryly observes, "The concept of box furniture received national publicity from hobby writer A. Neely Hall, who included chapters on the process in two of his books (although

© The Author(s) 2019
A. LaFarge, *Louise Brigham and the Early History of Sustainable Furniture Design*,
https://doi.org/10.1007/978-3-030-32341-7_6

he neglected to credit the technique to Brigham)."[2] Hall may have felt that Brigham was treading in his territory since his 1905 book *The Boy Craftsman* showed several points of kinship with *Box Furniture*. For one of Hall's larger pieces (a couch), he used whole boxes as an invisible understructure, and he also suggests such reuse ideas as turning thread spools into uprights for a hanging bookshelf.[3] In a 1915 issue of *St. Nicholas* in which Brigham published an article about box furniture, there is also an article by Hall about how to build a small toboggan slide out of packing cases.[4] It falls immediately after Brigham's article, which can hardly be an accidental placement.

Toward the end of World War I, Brigham finally began training young women in carpentry, through a school she set up at 16 Horatio Street in Greenwich Village.[5] One of Brigham's few commercial ventures, the school featured an associated store where toys made out of scrap wood were sold to passersby. Brigham organized a special summer course at her school to prepare the young women to take part in postwar relief efforts. The idea was that they would take their tools to Europe and teach soldiers recovering from injuries to make furniture from the sturdy packing crates that were being used to ferry war supplies to Europe.[6] In France and elsewhere, factories had stopped producing furniture during the war, leaving no easy way for soldiers returning home to quickly refurnish their plundered homes. Box furniture offered a practical solution to this problem.

Much like the restricted role that girls played in the HTA, these women were being trained in a support role—valuable on an interim basis until the economy got back to 'normal' and men returned to the workforce. Brigham undoubtedly understood that there was not yet any clear path for women to become professional carpenters or woodworkers, but she may also have felt that once women had acquired such skills, possibilities might open up. Not least, skilled women might form their own businesses, following the model of something like Maria Longworth Storer's Rookwood Pottery, the most famous of a group of nineteenth-century ceramics firms founded and run by women.

Brigham also started a box furniture factory on the Lower East Side in an attempt to capitalize on the growing demand for factory-made furniture.[7] Raising capital with the help of Home Thrift Association supporters, she acquired machinery and lumber and by 1915 had formed the Home Art Masters company. Her HTA assistant Ralph Albertson agreed to manage the factory and found a building to rent in Greenwich Village that would accommodate both factory and showroom.[8] This factory can be seen as a recognition on Brigham's part that teaching working people to make their own furniture runs up against a hard fact: many working people had very limited amounts of free time. Most of the box furniture factory labor thus ended up being provided by HTA apprentices. This was a period when more than one in every five boys aged 11 to 15 years was in the workforce, so it would not then have been seen by most people as an abuse of child labor but rather as an education in both carpentry and life skills.[9] The box furniture factory thus had the potential to give people jobs while still fulfilling those parts of Brigham's program that were about keeping costs low and reducing waste. Brigham eventually turned her factory over to the Bowery Branch of the YMCA specifically to help war veterans in need of jobs and job training.[10] This probably happened in response to two events in 1918: new regulations issued by the War Industries board controlling raw materials and setting production quotas, and passage of the Smith-Hughes Act, which appropriated federal funds for vocational instruction for returning servicemen.

Through a mail-order catalog, Home Art Masters offered furniture kits at moderate prices. This proto-IKEA furniture was mailed to the purchaser as a set of parts, which the company promised could be "quickly put together and finished. Everything including instructions, furnished. A boy or girl can set it up."[11] Brigham appears to have copyrighted the catalog for her ready-to-assemble furniture in 1915 as *Louise Brigham's I-Ma-Da Furniture*, though it is unclear if she actively used this punning name in the business.[12]

A Home Art Masters ad in the socialist magazine *The Masses* pictured a child's dressing stand, "the invention of Louise Brigham, famous for her original home furniture" (Fig. 6.1). It looks very much like a slight redesign of the Invalid's Bed Table (#78) from *Box Furniture*. It's worth quoting this ad at some length because it is practically the only place where Brigham praises herself as a designer:

> Women are delighted with this new invention.... Miss Brigham is a furniture genius, with hundreds of unique pieces. Send for her catalog, FREE. It reads like a fairy story to mothers and to those who want unique and serviceable furniture at amazingly low prices — less than half what you would pay for the shoddy, poor stuff in the stores.

Notably absent in the Home Art Masters materials I have seen is any reference to packing crates or box furniture. It seems probable that the factory

> # Price, $2.00
>
> ## A Child's Dressing Stand
>
> The invention of Louise Brigham, famous for her original home furniture. You will certainly want this most useful and unique nursery invention.
>
> Children's clothes either go on a chair, foot of the bed or floor. Children are easily taught to hang their clothes on this neat rack. It holds everything—even the contents of your boy's pockets. Women are delighted with this new invention. Send only $2. It will come in parts, quickly put together and finished. Everything, including instructions, furnished. A boy or girl can set it up. If, for any reason, a piece is damaged, we will replace it. Miss Brigham is a furniture genius, with hundreds of unique pieces. Send for her catalog, FREE. It reads like a fairy story to mothers and to those who want unique and serviceable furniture at amazingly low prices—less than half what you would pay for the shoddy, poor stuff in the stores. Send for catalog today and have your eyes opened to a new furniture world.
>
> *Send Orders to*
>
> ## HOME ART MASTERS, Inc.
> 140 FIFTH AVENUE, NEW YORK

Fig. 6.1 An ad for Home Art Masters kit furniture in *The Masses*, July 1915 (Image courtesy of HathiTrust and the Labadie Collection at the University of Michigan)

furniture was made using commercial lumber in order to justify the prices asked. This may also be why the ad does not indicate what kind of wood the dressing stand is made from—it would have been made from whatever wood was available during the war rather than from packing crates.[13]

Most design histories place the origin of modern ready-to-assemble (RTA) or flat-pack furniture around 1950. The Australian designer Frederick Ward started a mail-order RTA furniture business in the late 1940s, inspired like Brigham by a lack of affordable modern furniture for the working class.[14] In America, Ohio cabinetmaker Erie Sauder got the first U.S. patent for RTA furniture in 1953 for what he called a snap-together table designed to be assembled by the purchaser without need for either nails or glue.[15] In Europe, IKEA got into selling its furniture as flat-packs in 1956.

The roots of RTA furniture go much further back, however. For centuries people have made individual items of furniture designed to disassemble for ease of use or simpler and safer transport; examples include the trestle tables of medieval Europe, the portable furnishings of nomadic peoples worldwide, and the collapsible and folding furniture made for soldiers, sailors, colonizers, naturalists, and campers.[16] In many cases these, like the Sauder table, were designed around peg systems and other methods that avoided the problems posed by nails, screws, and glue. By the nineteenth century, there are examples of domestic furniture that was made in one place and then shipped in parts to be assembled at the other end by a local carpenter or shop.[17] For example, in 1830 the British architect Augustus Pugin designed a sideboard for a Mrs. Gough in Warwickshire that he sent flat-packed, with numbered parts and instructions, from London. He told Mrs. Gough that the piece was made in such a way that her carpenters would not need to use any glue.[18]

As these examples show, most ready-to-assemble domestic furniture made for fixed dwellings before the twentieth century consisted of one-off designs for individual buyers like Mrs. Gough. Brigham may have been the first person to create an entire business around selling ready-to-assemble household furniture directly to consumers through mass marketing. What inspired her to do so in the absence of obvious contemporary models is unclear. The portable housing that she lived in on Svalbard is a clear precursor, and it is possible that she encountered information about the portable dwellings of the Sami people during her travels in Scandinavia in the same period. It also seems likely that she would have drawn inspiration from the burgeoning contemporary industry of kit houses. Starting around 1900, a couple of dozen American manufacturers—the best known being Sears,

Roebuck—sold kit houses, shipping the numbered parts from the lumber mills to the buyers, to be built by local labor. The likeliest source of inspiration, however, is her Tak-Apart camp furniture from around 1914, just a year or so before she launched Home Art Masters.

Home Art Masters appears not to have survived very long nor to have made any lasting impact on the public. It would be another 30 years before RTA furniture began to catch the public imagination. Meantime, after a decade of sustained creative and entrepreneurial activity, Brigham's life began to move in unanticipated directions.

Notes

1. "Making Box Furniture," 218–221.
2. Gelber, *Hobbies*, 213.
3. Hall, *Boy Craftsman*, 63, 68. See also Hall's book *Handicrafts for Handy Boys*, 160–169.
4. Hall, "Small Toboggan Slide," 245–247.
5. Griswold, "What Women Are Doing."
6. Apparently, some time earlier Brigham had abandoned the use of packing crate material when crates began to be made out of "thin wood, bound together with wire bands," shifting for awhile to ordinary lumber. The better-made crates of the war years, which had to stand up to international shipment, allowed a return to the use of crates as raw material. Griswold, "What Women Are Doing."
7. "Educational" column, 315.
8. Kallman, "Pilgrimage of Ralph Albertson," 386–387. "Educational" column (315) lists Albertson as a partner, along with Arthur S. Levy, who was secretary of the dry goods firm Albertson, Beckhard and Allen, a New York company of which Albertson was president.
9. Leavitt, *Catharine Beecher to Martha Stewart*, 76; Zeisel, "Workweek in American Industry," 146.
10. "Educational" column, 315.
11. Home Art Masters advertisement, *The Masses*, 27.
12. Library of Congress Copyright Office, *Catalogue of Copyright Entries*, 1418.
13. There may also be some kind of link to the school and store on Horatio Street; at least one source lists 16 Horatio St. as the address for ordering a Home Art Masters catalog.
14. Cuffley, *Australian Houses*; Carter, "Blueprint to Patterncraft."
15. Combs, "Sauder to Offer Replica"; Forster, *Backroads & Byways of Ohio*.
16. For more on collapsible and portable furniture, see Giedion, *Mechanization Takes Command*.

17. There are a few earlier examples, such as eighteenth-century lacquered chairs made in China and disassembled into flat-packs for shipping to Great Britain, but these are quite rare before the nineteenth century. Personal communication from the Furniture History Society.
18. Hill, *God's Architect*, 85.

CHAPTER 7

Vanishing Act

Abstract This chapter assesses the period after World War I when the Progressive Era designer and social activist Louise Brigham slowly slid out of public view. Her marriage to retired Cleveland steel executive Henry Arnott Chisholm in 1916 may have factored into this transition, but it is also likely that her box furniture did not align well with the emerging values of convenience, ease, speed, and glamor that became design hallmarks of the 1920s. At some point, probably in the 1920s, Brigham worked on a planned 4th edition of her book *Box Furniture* that was never completed.

Keywords Louise Brigham · Marriage · Henry Arnott Chisholm

After World War I, Brigham and *Box Furniture* start to disappear from the cultural radar. The Winterthur Library holds a copy of the 1919 edition of *Box Furniture* annotated by Brigham, evidently in anticipation of a revised edition that never went to press (Fig. 7.1).[1] In these notes we see Brigham wearing all three of her hats: carpenter, social worker, and designer. In her extensive revision to the book's list of recommended tools, we see the first two at work. Half a dozen specialized tools are eliminated, as is her former use of brand names.[2] Most tellingly, nearly every tool is re-specified as to its size or gauge. For example, in place of a Barber's No. 223 8-inch brace, she specified simply an 11-inch brace. Cost is still on her mind: written

© The Author(s) 2019
A. LaFarge, *Louise Brigham and the Early History of Sustainable Furniture Design*,
https://doi.org/10.1007/978-3-030-32341-7_7

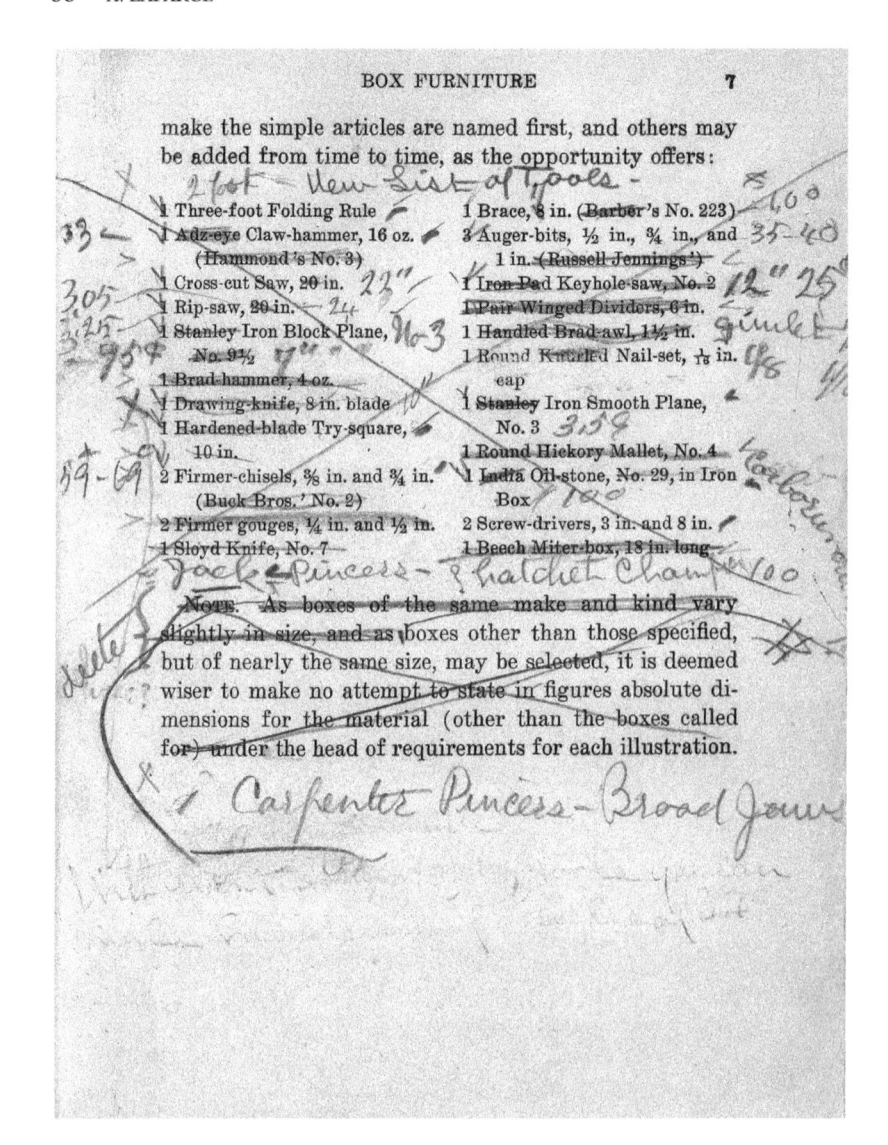

Fig. 7.1 Brigham's annotated list of tool changes in a copy of the 1919 edition of *Box Furniture* (Photo courtesy of the Winterthur Library: Printed Book and Periodical Collection)

in the margins of the revised list are estimated costs of the various tools. Smooth plane, $3.59. Ripsaw, $3.05. Brace, $1. Bits, 35–40 cents apiece.

Elsewhere in the revision notes, though, we see the designer at work: in two places she demands a "clearer blue" for the frontispiece. She simplifies the cover design, cutting out the two lamps and four small boxes that crowd the title. We also see her awareness of changing fashions: the word "shirtwaist" is to be changed throughout to "blouse," while "den" becomes "reception room." In one of the only uses of the word "modern" in anything Brigham said about her own work, there is a note to change the Octagon Nursery Table to a Modern Nursery Table.

Brigham's disappearance from public view may have been partly due to the many dislocations brought about by World War I. For one thing, her project may have fallen victim to the changing discourse around domestic values. As the field of advertising developed in the 1910s and 1920s, the word "convenience" began to be presented to women as an important value, displacing efficiency and frugality, both of which were watchwords for Brigham. (In 1929, she told an interviewer who was impressed with her ability to retrofit apartment closets as kitchens and bathrooms that efficiency was "the most important thing in life."[3]) Convenience as a concept makes it easier to throw things away because it suggests that housewives should be freed from annoying, time-consuming forms of work such as repair and remaking. Susan Strasser observes that "modern products offered release from the responsibility of caring for material goods, the stewardship of objects and materials that characterized the traditional relationship to the material world."[4] In the same period, production of machine-made furniture ramped up and critics increasingly praised such furniture for its perfection of fabrication—for the sleek surfaces in materials such as metal and bakelite that became hallmarks of 1920s design.

Thus did Brigham's project—labor-intensive, handmade, and thrift-oriented—find itself out of tune with the zeitgeist. All along, it had been easier for newspaper writers to address her work primarily as a social experiment or as amateur craftwork rather than as a fully modernist design project. With the postwar shift to valuing convenience, ease, speed, and glamor—the hallmarks of the Roaring Twenties—Brigham's geometric aesthetic became functionally invisible behind the low-tech craftsmanship and shoddy materials of the individual pieces. Her work was thus never really written about in its own time as if it were in direct dialog with the highly crafted design work of contemporaries like Gustav Stickley. It wasn't until a designer with a substantial portfolio of well-made work, Gerrit Rietveld, took up the challenge of crate furniture in the 1930s that it became possible to see how implicit in Brigham's work was a more extreme version of modernist design than was visible at the time. And it is fair to say that the full implications of box furniture as accessible design for the working class—the path that leads to a viable RTA industry in the 1950s and ultimately to a business on the global scale of IKEA—may have been unthinkable to Brigham herself, given her stake in individual fabrication. Only in her Tak-Apart camp furniture and her abortive Home Art Masters enterprise do we find hints of Brigham thinking about what mass production of her designs might look like. What is certain is that she consistently chose not to change her work in ways that would have made it appealing to the moneyed classes and the critical tastemakers—for example, by having her designs remade in fine hardwoods with excellent craftsmanship and glossy finishes.

And then there is the fact that a new phase of Brigham's life opened in 1916: on August 21 of that year, at the age of 41, she got married at the Mission Inn in Riverside, California.[5] Her spouse was a former steel industry executive from Cleveland, Henry Arnott Chisholm, whose first wife, Gertrude, had died 18 months earlier. Chisholm, who was more than twenty years older than Brigham, brought to the marriage a son, Andre Tozier Chisholm, who was only four years younger than his new stepmother.[6]

Henry Arnott Chisholm (1851–1920) belonged to a family of very wealthy industrialists who had emigrated to Cleveland from Scotland by way of Canada. His father, William Chisholm I, founded and ran several steel companies, including the Chisholm Steel Shovel Works, and his namesake uncle Henry Chisholm founded the Cleveland Rolling Mill, which became one of the largest steel companies in America.

Henry Arnott Chisholm spent most of his career working in the family businesses, first at the Cleveland Rolling Mill and later at the Chisholm Steel Shovel Works, which was incorporated in 1910 as William Chisholm's Sons Company. He retired in 1912, but before that, he served as president and his son Andre as vice-president of the renamed company. Brigham met Henry back when she was establishing the Sunshine Cottage settlement house in Cleveland, becoming friends with both Henry and Gertrude, and he is said to have toured her showcase apartment in New York after the publication of *Box Furniture*.[7]

Louise Brigham and her husband moved to Cleveland, although she returned periodically to New York during World War I to work with wounded veterans and manage her businesses.[8] It's possible that Henry's business experience was a factor in Brigham's decision to open the box furniture factory and the mail-order company. However, in the rare instances when Brigham appears in the press after her marriage, it is mostly in the role of a society woman, a fundraiser for museums and charitable endeavors.[9] How much, if any, of this transformation was the result of her marriage is unclear, but it suggests that as the wife of a rich businessman, she was moving more in white-gloved social circles somewhat removed from those where she had formerly worked side by side with social workers, laborers, and children.

Unusually for the time, Brigham continued to use a version of her own name after her marriage. She styled herself Mrs. Louise Brigham Chisholm rather than Mrs. Henry Chisholm, although the latter style was far more common in her social circle. In the 1930s, for example, she is listed as Mrs. Louise Brigham Chisholm alongside Mrs. William K. Vanderbilt and Mrs. Daniel Guggenheim as a participant in a fund-raising bazaar to which she donated "oriental silks and embroideries, collected abroad."[10]

The marriage did not last very long: Chisholm, who loved to travel, died in Yokohama, Japan, in September 1920, just four years after their wedding. After her husband's death, Brigham moved back to New York, taking up residence in McDougall Alley in yet another apartment featuring box furniture and folk art (as well as a reindeer skin rug from Spitsbergen).[11] At the time, McDougall Alley was known as the "Art Alley de Luxe" as it was where such affluent artists as Gertrude Vanderbilt Whitney and Daniel Chester French had their studios or homes. During this period, Brigham entertained local artists on Sunday afternoons and continued to travel abroad. It was even said, rather improbably, that she was the first woman to enter the tomb of King Tutankhamun after its rediscovery in 1922.[12]

By the late 1920s, Brigham had left New York and was living near Waterford, Connecticut, where she was in correspondence with the educator Martha Berry, founder of a series of primary schools in Georgia intended for the children of poor farmers, as well as of a junior college that eventually evolved into today's four-year Berry College. It's unclear how they knew each other—though Berry actively solicited donations among New York's well-to-do—but Brigham apparently funded at least one residential cottage for Berry's schools.[13] In a 1928 letter thanking Brigham for this donation, Berry remarks that she is sorry Brigham won't be visiting the school again that year, suggesting that Brigham's connection to the school extended beyond the impersonality of writing a check.

At some point, Brigham returned to New York, but there is not much information about her life during the latter half of the 1920s. It was probably in this period that she met the person who would shape the final phase of her life: the psychic healer and clairvoyant Edgar Cayce.[14]

Notes

1. It is unclear when these annotations were made.
2. She similarly generalizes all the packing crate types: "condensed-milk box" is to become "rectangular box," "butter box" is to become "oblong box," and so on.
3. Thompson, "Louise Brigham," 205.
4. Strasser, *Waste and Want*, 182.
5. According to Sidney Kirkpatrick (personal communication), Edgar Cayce's eldest son, Hugh Lynn Cayce, believed Louise had once been married to a consul of Norway, which if true would make the marriage to Chisholm her second. However, no evidence has ever turned up to support this suggestion.
6. Details about the Chisholm family in this section can be found in "News from the Classes," 276, and Ingham, *Biographical Dictionary*, 155–156.
7. "Money and Art Happily Mated," 16; and personal communication from Sidney Kirkpatrick.
8. Thompson, in "Louise Brigham" (204), notes that Brigham was officially commended for providing occupational therapy to veterans.
9. For example, in 1918, Brigham is reported as loaning a sculpture by Anna Hyatt Huntington to the Cleveland Museum of Art. "Contemporary American Bronzes," 152.
10. "Pen and Brush Club." The president of the Pen and Brush Club in this period was the journalist Ida Tarbell.
11. Clarage, "Main Street Meditations," 20.
12. Thompson, "Louise Brigham," 205, citing a 1929 story in the Cleveland *Plain Dealer*.
13. Martha Berry to Louise Brigham Chisholm, April 7, 1928.
14. A 1940 letter in the Cayce archives indicates that one of Brigham's sisters was also in contact with Cayce. This would have been either Lucy or Anna Esther, the only two of her sisters to survive to adulthood. Both were still alive in the early 1940s.

CHAPTER 8

Caycean Disciple

Abstract This chapter surveys the period from the mid 1930s to the mid 1940s when the Progressive Era designer and social activist Louise Brigham became close to the healer and clairvoyant Edgar Cayce, his family, and his secretary Gladys Davis. Cayce gave Brigham a series of what he called "readings" on subjects ranging from her health to her supposed past lives, and these are examined closely for the details they reveal about her failing health, her financial situation, and especially her concern about her legacy as a designer and writer. Brigham's later-life turn toward the spiritual is also reflected in her association with Unity Church during World War II.

Keywords Louise Brigham · Edgar Cayce · Gladys Davis · Unity Church

Edgar Cayce was born in Kentucky in 1877, the son of farmers. In 1901, Cayce became convinced that he had been cured of a bad case of laryngitis through suggestions made to him under hypnosis, and he became interested in exploring the limits of healing through hypnosis (Fig. 8.1). He began to give "readings" of other people's ailments while in a hypnotic trance himself, and in 1925 he moved to Virginia Beach, Virginia, where he established a hospital and founded the Association for Research and Enlightenment (A.R.E.), which is still active. Although he never obtained

Fig. 8.1 Healer and clairvoyant Edgar Cayce, 1941 (Photo courtesy of Edgar Cayce Foundation)

a medical degree and subscribed to many unscientific ideas (such as reincarnation), he appears to have been a gifted natural diagnostician. As time went on, his readings tended to revolve around three main areas of inquiry: illness and healing, past lives, and spiritual purpose.

Although it is uncertain how Louise Brigham first came in contact with Cayce, she had developed a close relationship with him and his family by the mid 1930s. According to Cayce's biographer Sidney Kirkpatrick, she lived on and off with the Cayces between 1936 and 1940 and later bought property in Virginia Beach. Brigham didn't settle there herself but visited regularly to get psychic readings, to study in the Cayce archives, and to write a memoir (now, sadly, lost). Apparently this was something of a spiritual autobiography as its opening chapter jumped back 2000 years to describe how Brigham had been the daughter of a Bethlehem inn-keeper in a prior incarnation[1]—an idea Brigham picked up from her very first reading with Cayce, which took place in 1936.

Inspired by this past life, Brigham apparently visited the Holy Land several times and went so far as to research ancient clothing for Hebrew women. In later years, no matter where she found herself at Christmas, she would tell the story of Jesus's nativity while wearing her own version of that ancient costume, consisting of an ankle-length robe in mixed black and colored fabrics topped off by a headdress.[2] This latent and Orientalist theatricality is nowhere evident in earlier photographs. Brigham belonged to a generation of middle-class women who were taught to place a high value on being ladylike, and the few photographs of Brigham as a young adult suggest that she conformed to this in her clothing choices—we don't find her in bloomers. Even in staged pictures that show her using carpentry tools, we find her in a respectable, floor-length, plain dark dress, while an undated formal portrait shows her in a conventional Edwardian evening dress.

It is hard to find clear roots among her earlier writings and interviews for Brigham's late-in-life turn to spiritual inquiry. Almost certainly raised a Protestant,[3] she rarely referenced God or spiritual matters, and then only in conventional terms. For example, among the mottoes on the kitchen walls at Box Corner First were "The Crown of the House is Godliness" and "Who Sweeps a Room as to God's Praise Makes That and the Action Fine."[4]

Cayce gave Brigham 14 psychic readings between 1936 and 1942. In the records kept of these readings at the A.R.E., participants are generally identified by a code number rather than a name; Brigham was #1152. Cayce's secretary, Gladys Davis, recorded his readings in shorthand, and from these verbatim or near-verbatim transcripts, one can see that people brought him questions ranging from the urgent—Will this disease kill me? Should I marry X?—to the silly: Why do I feel that I was a great poet in my last incarnation? Can you tell me about my past life in Egypt... China... Greece... Atlantis?

The first reading for Brigham took place at a friend's apartment in New York on April 20, 1936. Cayce starts off talking about Brigham in characterological generalities as signified astrologically: the influence of Mercury in her life indicates "high mental ability," of Venus "affability," of Mars "anger." He asks of Brigham's relationship to God, "How close art thou to knowing His ways?" before moving on to her past lives, which he warns may be "few in number." It is at this point that Cayce informs "the entity" (his usual term for the subject of his readings) that she was once Jenife, the comely daughter of a Bethlehem inn-keeper—and not just any inn-keeper. Louise-Jenife, in the guise of a girl one year younger than the Virgin Mary, apparently "stood by" for Jesus's birth and thus became the second human being ever to hold the Christian savior in her arms.[5] A bit later, she witnessed the arrival of the three kings with their gifts. No wonder Brigham liked to retell the story of the Nativity at Christmastime: she had "witnessed" it firsthand.

Cayce greatly elaborated the story of Louise-Jenife's life during Brigham's third reading. Here her name is given by Cayce as Sarapha or Sara instead of Jenife, an inconsistency that Cayce's secretary Gladys Davis later attempted to explain away on various muddled grounds having to do with differences in "vibrations" and/or ancient languages. Among other matters, we learn that Jenife had been sought in marriage by a "registrar" whom she had rejected, and that this registrar was none other than Brigham's dead husband, Henry Chisholm, in a previous incarnation. Several past-life characters that Cayce had intuited for his sitters, including Jenife/Sara, were used by the writer Mary Lacroix in her 1989 novel *The Remnant*, which focuses on three Essene women preparing for the advent of the Messiah in ancient Palestine. Jenife/Sara's story is taken up in the third section of the book.[6]

After Cayce finished with his initial reading, Brigham was given permission to ask questions. The ones she chose for that first session revolved around classic writers' issues: Am I writing along the right lines, what causes blocks in my thoughts, what will clarify my writing, do I have the right collaborator? Cayce's answers mainly fall along spiritual lines and are rather opaque. To her question about writer's block he responded: "This has been given, in that way and manner in which ye may open thine self to the glories of the Most High." One of his clearest responses is to a question about *Box Furniture*.

(Q) Will my old book be used?
(A) In a revised manner, yes.

In most of her early readings, Brigham appears worried about health issues.[7] She asks about a pelvic hernia; about headaches, numbness, and excessive perspiration; about what sounds like a kidney stone and about black intestinal discharges.[8] She asks whether anything can be done about a painful "water tumor" in her pelvic region, to "dissolve the growth and eliminate it without an operation."[9] (Cayce apparently didn't think she had a tumor at all, linking her symptoms instead to gastrointestinal problems.)[10] Now in her early 60s, she asks how she might go about improving her memory and sharpening her ability to concentrate. Cayce sensibly recommends hydrotherapy, massage, laxatives, enemas, moderate walking, and a change in diet[11] oriented toward more whole grains, fibrous fruits and vegetables, and fluids. Sidney Kirkpatrick is of the opinion that Cayce's treatments may actually have saved Brigham's life: "For more than a decade she had been undergoing treatment for a severe gastrointestinal condition that the Cayce recommendations cleared up in a matter of weeks."[12] By June of 1939, Brigham was feeling so much better that she wrote Cayce as follows: "So much strength has returned of late that I have suddenly accepted an invitation with all my expenses paid to be the only New York delegate to San Francisco for the Convention of the National League of American Pen Women. I, being the second vice-president of the New York Branch, I am simply thrilled with delight."[13]

In two early readings, financial issues also surface.[14] Brigham asks if her recent decision to lease some property in Cleveland was correct and whether she has the right lawyer. By the fifth reading, in late 1937, she is wondering whether she should be disturbed by unspecified recent events that have greatly reduced her income. And she asks, too, about how she should handle a friendship that has gone sour.

Brigham's fourth reading, and all subsequent ones, took place in Virginia Beach. Here she asks a string of questions about her life's work and her writing: "Why am I so fond of carpentry and invention of furniture?.... Why am I so anxious to put into book form the mass of material I have not yet published?.... Is my material what the world needs, or wants?" Cayce's answer rambles but appears to connect Brigham's interest in carpentry to her past life in an inn taking care of people's need for rest and to the idea of dwelling places for the soul. Despite his vagaries, Cayce consistently encourages Brigham to continue with her autobiography, which at one point he suggests could even run to three volumes.[15] In her fifth reading Brigham asks: "If I finish [the autobiography], will it help get my other books published?", and in her ninth she asks about "unfinished books on my furniture (inventions or ideas)," indicating that she had more than one writing project in hand at this stage of her life and that she had not stopped thinking about furniture design.

Shortly after the outbreak of World War II, she asked Cayce for direction on serving humanity and inquired if there were a "definite work to perform throughout this world crisis." She asked about becoming affiliated with various groups and individuals: the British revivalist movement Moral Re-Armament, the Christian mystic Flower Newhouse, the Austrian social reformer Rudolf Steiner.[16] Brigham had been feeling for some time that she wanted to leave New York and repeatedly asked Cayce for guidance on subletting or getting rid of her apartment in the city and dispersing her manuscripts, her library, her furniture, her art objects.[17] She was experiencing a new set of physical symptoms—itching, sensations of ice water running down the legs—indicative of poor circulation.[18] From the pattern of Brigham's questions emerges the portrait of a woman who feels ungrounded, directionless, anxious, and yet also strongly interested in formalizing her legacy.

By the fall of 1941, it appears that Brigham was seriously contemplating a permanent move to Virginia Beach. By this time, she had become a stalwart supporter of Cayce's work (Fig. 8.2), having donated funds to build a fireproof vault that would protect Cayce's archives.[19] She referred many people to Cayce and in some cases funded their readings.[20] Brigham even bought a piece of property next door to Cayce's home and the A.R.E. headquarters with the idea of building a duplex. But by Christmas of 1941 she had changed her mind and instead gave the property to Gladys Davis, of whom she was especially fond. Her note read in part: "Gladys, dear girl, to you who for years have done so much to make our Readings possible to possess, and to preserve—ever willing and gracious to do your part—I am giving you this Christmas Day 'The Land'! 'Go In and Possess this Good Earth.'" Davis built a cottage on Brigham's Christmas gift in 1949 and lived there until the mid 1980s.[21]

At some point during World War II, Brigham became interested in Unity Church, an organization within the New Thought movement that promoted an idea of universal divinity. She visited the church's headquarters at what was then Unity Farm and is now Unity Village (a suburb of Kansas

Fig. 8.2 Louise Brigham (center) with Edgar Cayce's son Hugh Lynn Cayce (left) and Hugh's wife Sally (right), 1941 (Photo courtesy of Edgar Cayce Foundation)

City, Missouri).[22] She participated in their prayer program known as Silent Unity, working in the letter-writing department in July and August 1945 and refusing any pay for her work.[23] She lived in a Kansas City hotel during her stay rather than at Unity Farm itself. According to Gladys Davis, she was so happy there that she gave up any idea of returning to live in Virginia Beach. Eventually, she went back to New York instead.

By 1955, the hints of circulation and memory problems that appear in Brigham's later readings with Cayce had manifested in concrete forms. She had a heart attack, and she experienced a hardening of the arteries that affected her memory, probably through reduced blood flow.[24] A friend who visited her in the Sylvan Nursing Home in West Trenton, N.J., where she lived during the last few years of her life, reported sadly that although Brigham recognized her friend, she had completely forgotten about Cayce.[25] She died in the nursing home on March 30, 1956, aged 81.

Notes

1. Personal communication from Sidney Kirkpatrick.
2. Personal communication from Sidney Kirkpatrick.

3. The transcript of one of Brigham's psychic readings is annotated: "Widow, Writer, Protestant."
4. Brigham, "How I Furnished," Part IV, 68.
5. Edgar Cayce Readings 1152-1 and 1152-3, A.R.E. archives. Cayce goes on to say, in that same reading, that Louise had had yet *another* past life. In that one, she had been in Atlantis when it broke up and sank and had helped to save the lives of many people who escaped to other countries.
6. Edgar Cayce Reading 1152-3, A.R.E. archives.
7. Edgar Cayce Readings 1152-2 and 1152-5, A.R.E. archives.
8. Edgar Cayce Readings 1152-7 and 1152-8, A.R.E. archives.
9. Edgar Cayce Readings 1152-2 and 1152-5, A.R.E. archives.
10. Edgar Cayce Reading 1152-8, A.R.E. archives.
11. Edgar Cayce Reading 1152-5 and 1152-6, A.R.E. archives.
12. Personal communication from Sidney Kirkpatrick.
13. Report of Edgar Cayce Reading 1152-8. I have corrected here Louise's original misspelling of the organization's name as "Penwomen."
14. Edgar Cayce Readings 1152-2 and 1152-5, A.R.E. archives.
15. Edgar Cayce Readings 1152-4, A.R.E. archives.
16. Edgar Cayce Readings 1152-11, A.R.E. archives.
17. Edgar Cayce Readings 1152-10 and 1152-11, A.R.E. archives.
18. Edgar Cayce Readings 1152-11, A.R.E. archives.
19. Kirkpatrick and Kirkpatrick, "Louise Brigham."
20. Per 1939 letter from #1859 and 1941 letter from #2610 in the A.R.E. archives.
21. *Friends of the A.R.E. Library*, 4, and personal communication from Sidney Kirkpatrick.
22. Kirkpatrick believes she took with her to Unity Farm the manuscript of her autobiography, although Unity Church does not appear to have it in its archives.
23. Information from Unity librarian, forwarded by Sidney Kirkpatrick.
24. Report of Edgar Cayce Reading 1152-13, A.R.E. Archives. The phrase "hardening of the arteries" indicates that she likely suffered from atherosclerosis.
25. Report of Edgar Cayce Reading 1152-13, A.R.E. Archives.

CHAPTER 9

The Contemporary Context

Abstract This chapter assesses Progressive Era designer and social activist Louise Brigham as a progenitor of several strands of contemporary design, including sustainable and recycled-materials design, do-it-yourself design, modular and multifunctional design for apartments, and RTA and kit furniture design. Following an overview of how these areas of design developed over the last hundred years in Europe and the United States, the chapter takes up two examples of recent design projects to interrogate the ways in which contemporary design both reflects and diverges from Brigham's aesthetic and ethos. Finally, the chapter argues for Brigham as an exemplar of a form of "alternative modernity" that was radical for the unique ways that she took modernist ideas and refracted them through her own version of Progressive Era values.

Keywords Louise Brigham · Box furniture · Sustainable design · Do-it-yourself design · Green design · Modular furniture · Multifunctional furniture

Toward the end of a 1910 *New York Times* interview, Brigham uses a phrase that neatly summarizes the driving principle of her box furniture project: "The idea is not commercial so much as reciprocal."[1] She did not wish to be known as a charity worker[2]; rather, she saw herself as a champion

© The Author(s) 2019
A. LaFarge, *Louise Brigham and the Early History of Sustainable Furniture Design*,
https://doi.org/10.1007/978-3-030-32341-7_9

99

of Progressive Era ideals of utility, simplicity, frugality, efficiency, and self-education—both for herself and for others. Her entry in the 1939–1940 volume of a biographical dictionary of American women—for which she may have supplied the information herself—tags her as "inventor, lecturer, writer."[3]

One major cause of her obscurity, then, is likely the fact that she never fully saw herself as a designer—and no one else did either. Apart from her early studies in Europe and her connection to Hoffmann, Stickley, and Aschermann, she did not really travel in design circles. She took part in expositions oriented toward industrial arts in the broadest sense rather than in design-focused exhibits. Yet it would equally be a mistake to think there was nothing of the designer in Brigham and that her modernist aesthetic was an accidental side effect of her choice of packing crates as a material. In light of her acknowledgment that her entire system ultimately traces back to Hoffmann's square, that view is simply untenable.

Since Hoffmann and Brigham were near contemporaries—they also died within a few months of one another in 1956—it's instructive to consider their contrasting levels of success. This was an awkward transition period for American women artists and designers, with few highly influential figures emerging before the modernist cohort that is a generation or so younger than Brigham. In the furniture and interior design fields, it is often observed that nothing much happened between the late nineteenth century (heyday of the Arts and Crafts movement, Art Nouveau, and Mission styles) and the 1920s, when De Stijl caught on partly as a consequence of the 1925 Paris International Exposition of Modern Industrial and Decorative Arts.[4] In America, as the Arts and Crafts movement and Mission styles were fizzling out, we find mainly a few devotees of the Wiener Werkstätte aesthetic such as the German Winold Reiss, who immigrated in 1913 and whose 1915 interior for the Busy Lady Baking Company displays a spare geometric aesthetic loosely akin to Brigham's. McClain and Long write of the Aschermanns: "Though they had attracted considerable attention with their work, [their] impact on the rise of modern American design was fleeting. They were perhaps too far ahead of their time: their work had all but been eclipsed before the modern movement had regained momentum in the United States in the mid-1920s."[5]

This summary applies to the proto-modernist Brigham as well. If she had been born just slightly later, it's entirely possible that she would have ended up with a more typical designer's career—perhaps something akin to that of the Bauhaus textile designer Anni Albers (born 1899), the textile

Fig. 9.1 Gerrit Rietveld's Crate Chair, ca. 1934 (Photo courtesy of Brooklyn Museum, gift of Rosemarie Haag Bletter and Martin Filler, 1994.160. Creative Commons-BY [Photo: Brooklyn Museum, CUR.1994.160.jpg])

and furniture designer Ilonka Karasz (b. 1896), or the Austrian architect-designer Margarete Schütte-Lihotzky (b. 1897), whose Taylorist "Frankfurt Kitchen" shows a number of affinities with Brigham's work.

Apart from the Wiener Werkstätte, the first design movement to show a close alliance with Brigham's ultra-plain geometry is De Stijl, which emerged in 1917 in Europe. One of its leaders was the Dutch designer Gerrit Rietveld, whose geometric design sensibility has some kinship with Brigham's although he was more than a decade younger. Like Brigham, Rietveld was driven by a desire to make well-designed objects cheaper and more widely available. In the mid-1930s, he designed several pieces of furniture from raw wood, including a bookcase, a small table, and (most famously) a 1934 armchair that became canonized in design history as the Crate Chair (Fig. 9.1). Although it's often said that they were made from recycled packing crates, in actual fact they were made from the same *kind* of cheap spruce wood used to construct such crates.[6] Rietveld preferred them raw so that their origins were visible, but they were often painted by their owners.[7] The final appearance of these pieces was largely determined by the fact that they were built from standard 6-inch-wide planks that were screwed together but left unglued at the joints. The rough-carpentry aesthetic was criticized in some circles as a lack of traditional craftsmanship, but Rietveld argued—in a truly Brighamesque spirit—that his intention was to honor the materiality of the wood itself.

Although in aesthetic, materials, and construction, Rietveld's crate furniture is a near relative of Brigham's box furniture, it is important not to elide the differences. For one thing, Brigham was always focused on making furniture that was easy to live with, while Rietveld was making an aesthetic statement that took the form of furniture. And there are no really close cognates between his crate-based designs and any individual pieces of Brigham's box furniture, though the Crate Table bears some affinities with Brigham's Flower Stand (#35) and Dressing Table (#79). The fact remains that the design world was not ready for the aesthetics of crate furniture in 1909—it would be barely ready in 1935—and such acceptance as Brigham found came mainly under the banners of education and thrift. When crate furniture does come into view in the design world with Rietveld's Crate Chair, the most impressive elements in Brigham's program—the reskilling of the working class, the do-it-yourself ethos, the social goal of reducing waste—are almost entirely absent.[8]

World War II interrupted and shifted the development of design in the United States. Despite the direction suggested by Rietveld's crate furniture, it isn't until the late 1950s that a programmatic use of recycled and sustainable materials in design and architecture begins to take off with the work of visionary architects like Paolo Soleri and the team of Michael Kahn and Leda Livant, as well as the efforts of amateur builders working with salvaged materials.[9] This trend resonates with what was going on in the field of fine art, where artists like Eva Hesse and Jean Tinguely were using industrial castoffs as their raw materials. In the 1970s, the Italian designer Enzo Mari published an influential book entitled *Autoprogettazione* (loosely, "Self Design") in which he discussed craftsmanship in ways that Brigham would have appreciated: he saw making as a journey that develops self-knowledge and design knowledge alongside skills.[10] The book included a range of very plain furniture designs that could be built with the most limited of materials and tools (hammer, nails, ordinary boards). These developments in turn point toward the do-it-yourself and maker movements of the 1990s and early 2000s. Brigham's Gracie

Mansion workshop was a direct predecessor of today's many hundreds of makerspaces and open workshops such as New York's Seaport Community Tool Library, as well as (though more indirectly) of the vast library of YouTube videos through which people can learn a wide array of artisanal skills by watching experts at work.

It is also not until after World War II that modular and multifunctional furniture becomes widely popular, reflecting "a departure from the static modern interior and a return to the 18th century concept of rooms with multiple uses."[11] But this postwar furniture is again designed primarily for the middle class. It isn't until quite recently that one finds designers working extensively with ideas of modularity and multifunctionality as well as a target audience of deskilled urbanites living in very small apartments and without much disposable income. In the last decade or so, there has been a convergence between the DIY and maker movements and the open design movement, which aims to enable adaptable designs and encourage local production of goods, both of which are values very evident in Brigham's box furniture project. Objects made out of unusual recycled materials are now commonplace among both amateur and professional designers. To cite only a couple of pertinent examples, in Brazil designers like Augusto Cintrangulo are making toys and musical instruments from commercial packaging, and there is a website dedicated to sharing ways to rebuild and repurpose IKEA furniture.[12] There is a broad embrace of qualities Brigham would have appreciated: uncomplicated form, repurposed materials, and visible traces of the original source. One major difference, of course, is that a great deal of today's open design depends on computers, from the design of the objects, to the way they are shared over the internet, to the fabrication (at least in part) using various computer-aided technologies like 3D printing and laser-cutting.

To further illuminate some of the connections between contemporary design and Brigham's work, I want to look more closely at the work of two designers who carry forward Brigham's ideas in different ways. Around 2010, the Laotian-German architect Van Bo Le-Mentzel started designing furniture for very small (225-square-foot) studio apartments.[13] He has been publishing the designs for free on his company website, Hartz IV Möbel, so that apartment dwellers can build their own furniture (Fig. 9.2). Bauhaus-inspired in form, the pieces are designed to be easy to build out of ordinary, commercially available wood with few tools. There are half a dozen designs, and several pieces are multipurpose. The resulting furniture looks a great deal like Brigham's would if it were remade using the same materials.

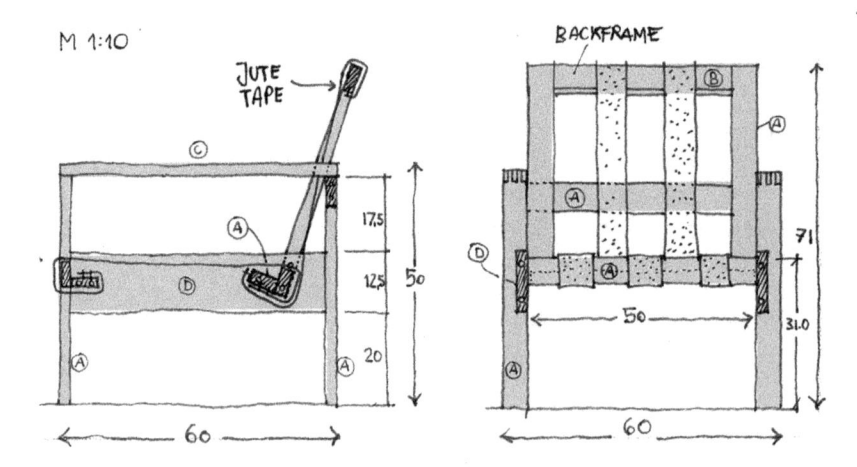

Fig. 9.2 A detail of Van Bo Le-Mentzel's schematic for version 3 of his 24-Euro Chair (Image courtesy of the artist)

One point of departure from Brigham's box furniture project (apart from the materials used) is Le-Mentzel's target audience of Millennials: although economically squeezed, they are generally better off than Brigham's turn-of-the-century tenement dwellers. Being able to afford a studio apartment in a European or American city in 2012 positions you as someone who has moved up from sharing an apartment or living at home. One writer's description of Le-Mentzel's project as a "democratic takeover of the good life"[14] makes the point neatly: this is furniture that plays to aspirations for upward mobility rather more than to stark utility. The plans themselves are informally drawn (some with bilingual German/English instructions), and like many things shared on the internet in the 2010s, they have a distinct flavor of self-promotion. One version of the plan, for instance, is entitled "The Legendary 24-Euro Chair."[15]

Around the same time, designer Farah Nasser (then a graduate student at Purdue University) undertook a field study to design multifunctional furniture for a refugee camp in Jordan. The goal was to "maximize space usage and improve the livelihood conditions of people living in underprivileged communities."[16] Among the pieces she designed were storage, seating, a table, and sleeping units. Her design criteria prioritized being "easy-to-implement and aesthetically pleasing" (Fig. 9.3).[17] She also planned on a manufacturing process that would be led by local people, and to this end

Fig. 9.3 Farah Nasser's rendering of her multifunctional furniture designs, 2013 (Image courtesy of the artist)

she produced diagrams and graphics. She specified that the raw materials should be readily available, inexpensive, and reasonably durable. Nasser explicitly grounds her approach in the "cradle to cradle" ethos of architect William McDonough and chemist Michael Braungart. Although she does not use upcycled materials, she is attentive to the environmental and social implications of choosing one local material over another. We can see in her project what Finnish writer Tommi Laitio has identified as a shift in the role of the designer "toward the roles of a trainer, translator, and integrator"—which is not entirely dissimilar to how Brigham might have seen herself.[18]

Nasser began by asking whether "sustainably developed multifunctional furniture [could] benefit underprivileged communities."[19] She went on to survey the specific needs of the refugees with whom she planned to work. Although the actual survey work done was minimal (amounting to one week of research in the target community), this approach still differs from that of Brigham's day, when designers and reformers tended to assume they knew what was needed from their more educated perspective and would almost certainly not have carried out a formal survey of the needs of a target population (although informal consultations probably took place). As one 1905 writer put it: "By means of the Model Flat the settlement workers have undertaken to solve some of the problems of the tenement."[20] The reformers of Brigham's day were not asking whether their ideas *could* benefit the tenement dwellers; rather, they began by assuming their ideas *would* be of benefit.

I have described this project at some length because of the many ways in which it echoes Brigham's project. Like Brigham, Nasser started with a trio of related hopes: that her multifunctional furniture would make living conditions better, that it would promote a sense of self-worth because people would build the furniture themselves, and that it would develop marketable skills among those who chose to make the furniture. In addition (and unlike Brigham), she hoped to stimulate the local economy through marketing surplus items to neighboring countries. It also represents one among a growing number of architectural and furniture design projects aimed at assisting the world's many displaced peoples; another example is the award-winning Better Shelter project set up as a partnership between IKEA and the United Nations High Commissioner for Refugees (UNHCR).[21] However, nothing in the thesis suggests that Nasser's furniture was ever built, even in prototype form—a necessary step toward working out the kinds of design flaws that only appear under conditions of actual use. By contrast, both Le-Mentzel and Brigham's designs have been refined through actual use; Le-Mentzel has published at least three versions of his 24-Euro Chair, while Brigham's designs underwent endless retesting in the Gracie Mansion workshop and in her own apartments, and she published several editions of her book.

It is important not to lose sight of the fact that Brigham was as much of her time as she was ahead of it. Furniture design and craftwork are often seen as traditional because of the way that they value familiar forms and kinds of functionality. Certainly, Brigham's design work can be seen in this light, as her furniture designs are all variations on what would have been found in any American home of her day: desks, bookshelves, tables, chairs, and so on. Furniture on the whole evolves rather slowly, alongside social evolution rather than ahead of it. The areas where design can be progressive or anti-traditional also evolve. It can push back against the standardization and cheap materials of mass production, for instance; a stance epitomized by the Arts and Crafts movement. Brigham's work cuts across this position in an interesting way. She champions standardization and cheap production but as a means to individual production rather than to mass manufacture. She saw that her designs, standardized on available cheap materials, offered an opening to hand-crafting that would not otherwise be available to the urban working class.

Brigham was not the kind of reformer who looks only backward to an era when everything was better, and who strives for some kind of return to a lost golden age. Nor was she a reformer in the William Morris mold; most of her rhetoric is not aimed against industrialism per se; she was advocating for self-reliance rather than a change in social conditions. Moreover, she adhered to the early modernist principles of her day—simplicity, geometry, rectilinearity, avoidance of ornament—that many traditionalists roundly rejected. The main area where she can be seen to support traditional values is in her championship of European handicrafts, many of which she had learned during her educational tours abroad and which she wrote about in some of her interior design articles for *Ladies' Home Journal*. Even here, her attention is focused largely on how to help immigrant women make a living from their handicraft skills, rather than on putting these forms of art forward as aesthetically better than anything else. She would likely have found herself in sympathy with today's fair trade movement, aimed at sustaining traditional handicrafts worldwide through ensuring better economic conditions for those producing such goods.

Within those limitations, Brigham was nonetheless remarkably visionary: her box furniture is one of the earliest design projects to incorporate the idea of modular or sectional units, to focus specifically on the use of recycled materials, and to organize an entire design program around a primarily social rather than a strictly aesthetic objective. In addition, she may have been the first person to set up a mail-order, direct-to-consumers, ready-to-assemble furniture business. Taken together, these aspects of Brigham's work place her as a direct precursor of today's do-it-yourself and low-impact design movements, as well as of consumer-assembled kit furniture such as IKEA produces. Furniture made out of recycled materials is now in the mainstream of contemporary design.

Brigham was also unusual for her *systematic* approach to design: both in the systematizing of process (modular furniture constructed of predetermined units of material) and in the holistic approach to design goals: an entire apartment's worth of furniture whose aesthetic demanded a minimal use of materials. As architect Daniel Williams points out, "Sustainable designs are *system designs*. They help solve the economic, social, and environmental issues *simultaneously* and as a single system."[22] Brigham's approach adds up to just such a sustainable design system. Her work implicated all three of the areas of concern to the field of sustainable design:

economy, environment, and community. With respect to the economy, she contributed by leveraging the limited resources of the working class, effectively helping them to raise their standard of living. With respect to the environment, box furniture meant less cutting of new wood and less wastage of old wood, both by limiting the amounts thrown away and by making a given amount of wood stretch further through the use of a stripped-down aesthetic. And finally, with respect to the community, she brought modern design to a class that otherwise could not have afforded it, as well as skills training that would not otherwise have been available. When she wrote that her goal was "beautiful homes for all," she really meant it.[23]

In the twentieth century, some opponents of modernism set themselves against what has been called "the authoritarian dream of total design."[24] In her systematizing approach, Brigham was arguably dreaming a dream of total design—and yet it is impossible to figure this as springing from an authoritarian or ideological impulse. There is a pragmatism at the heart of Brigham's project that militates against a totalizing point of view: her system is *good enough* for what it offers, but it is essentially a stopgap. It wouldn't be needed by workers who could earn enough more money to either buy a better grade of furniture or learn to make it in a woodworking class, nor would it be needed in quite the same way in a world that had figured out how to get cheap but well-designed and sustainably made furniture into the hands of the working class. Although we now live in a world of readily available, well-designed mass-produced furnishings, these are still priced for an economic stratum (middle and upper working class) somewhat above where Brigham was aiming her efforts. Moreover, with most such furniture, there remains the thorny question of how to make it with less waste of resources and how to dispose of it when it is worn out or broken down. Brigham's project thus remains one possible answer to a question design historian Tanya Harrod poses: "Why make art at all in such a full world?"[25] There is always the possibility of modeling a better way of doing things.

Today, not a single piece of Brigham's furniture is known to have survived,[26] and until recently her box furniture project was all but unknown. This question of survival is nontrivial, as the lack of preserved objects makes it enormously more difficult to study her life and work. It is a fact that under capitalism, objects made by women have been generally less often saved and archived than those made by men, and this would be even more the case for Brigham's box furniture, whose shoddiness of materials would make it harder for anyone to see them as storehouses of value and thus worth saving.[27]

Brigham's ideas seem not to have been picked up by any other designers of her day or in subsequent decades, with the possible exception of a few home economists here and there such as Altha Tedrow. Although Brigham's obituary in the *New York Times* does state that her work "was said to have influenced the development of some modern styles in furniture,"[28] and another article observed that "in the art of America, hers has become an epoch,"[29] I haven't yet found any designer who acknowledged her influence.

That picture began to change in the 1990s, when Brigham initially emerged from the footnotes of design history through the scholarship of Neville Thompson.[30] A few years later a pair of blog posts by Jessica Pigza and Larry Weinberg offered informal appreciations of Brigham's work in light of contemporary design movements heavily focused on sustainability, the handmade, and low cost.[31] Yet the differences between Brigham's project and contemporary design remain as important as the similarities. While Brigham's do-it-yourself approach had much in common with today's low-impact movement, it is by no means identical. She never explicitly argued for recycling used materials as a matter of ecological principle, as one might today; instead, she took the ethical position that waste of any kind is immoral. Her program was also explicitly oriented toward assisting the working poor by making it possible for them to build well-designed furnishings "at minimum expense" from cast-off materials.[32] As a reskilling program, it differs somewhat from today's DIY, "maker" and artisanal aesthetics, which are as often geared toward the middle class as the working class, with an underlying program that has as much to do with raising property values and demonstrating social status through acquired skills as with saving money or improving domestic functionality. Indeed, it is remarkable that despite her evident interest in works of high craftsmanship, Brigham dedicated her best efforts not to developing programs to encourage highly skilled handicrafts like lacemaking or weaving as forms of small business—although she did that, too—but instead to getting "the most out of the means at hand"[33] through inculcation of minimal skills and a correspondingly bare-bones aesthetic program.[34] Though today we notice the datedness of the language in which she speaks earnestly of "peasants" and the "humble classes," the fact remains that she spent her entire career working with and for people of small means instead of chasing the luxury trade that was then, and remains today, the only sure way to make a name for yourself in the field of design.

When Brigham asked Edgar Cayce, "Why am I so fond of carpentry and invention of furniture?", one notices not just that the question is unanswerable, but that it was asked at all. There is something almost desperate in this question, as if she is asking about a forbidden desire; it is not an expression of self-regard, pride, or happiness. Brigham's life exhibits in full the paradox of her time: talented women trying to make their way in the "male" sphere of work, but segregated into those areas of design considered appropriate—which did not include furniture design and woodworking, for the most part—and encouraged mainly in the spheres of "feminine" handicrafts, domestic economy, social work, and education. One could even point to a certain irony in the fact that her furniture designs, so perfectly fulfilling Adolf Loos's masculinist prescription of a style stripped of ornamentation, should have been largely ignored by the leading male designers of the day, with the notable exceptions of Hoffmann, Stickley, and Aschermann.

At the same time, there is no good reason to try to squeeze Brigham fully into the box of modernist design and avant-garde thinking; she was too much the Progressive Era reformer and educator. To borrow a phrase, her practice might best be seen as a kind of "alternative modernity."[35] Her interpretation of modernism turned out to be radical in its own way for how it refracted modernist aesthetics through an ethical lens, leading to what would now be called a social practice. Her work exemplifies the ways in which design is "a process of representation" whose objects embody cultural values and aspirations.[36] As the design historian Pat Kirkham writes, Brigham "provides a quintessential example of a life devoted to addressing William Morris's question, 'What business have we with art at all, unless we can share it?'"[37] In the end, it is for being a living embodiment of this spirit that Louise Brigham most deserves to be remembered.

Notes

1. "Exhibition to Aid Home Industries," 10.
2. "Miracles with Old Boxes," 3.
3. Howes, *American Women*, 164.
4. McClain and Long, "Aschermanns"; Harrod, *Real Thing*, 149. The picture is slightly different in architecture, where the aesthetic of the Prairie School

and the work of Frank Lloyd Wright in particular offered more of a throughline into the De Stijl and Bauhaus aesthetics that arrived in the United States in the 1920s and 1930s.
5. McClain and Long, "Aschermanns."
6. Russell, *Century of Chair Design*, 107.
7. The Crate Chair is now available in several versions and colors as an assemble-it-yourself kit.
8. Rietveld apparently wanted to sell his crate chair as a DIY kit, but his buyers weren't interested. See Richardson, *102 Midcentury Chairs*.
9. Examples include Soleri's desert town of Arcosanti, or Kahn and Levant's compound known as Eliphante, both in Arizona. For more on salvage architecture, see Adamson, *Thinking Through Craft*, 89–95; Jencks and Silver, *Adhocism*.
10. Mari, *Autoprogettazione*.
11. Fitzgerald, *American Furniture*, 500.
12. Van Abel et al., *Open Design*, 216, 223.
13. Hagel, "Democratic Design."
14. Christine McLaren, "Hartz IV Möbel."
15. This is the equivalent of about $1 in 1910.
16. Nasser, "Multifunctional Furniture," xii.
17. Nasser, "Multifunctional Furniture," xiii.
18. Laitio, "Best Design to Just Design," 195.
19. Nasser, "Multifunctional Furniture," xiii.
20. Smith, "Gospel of Simplicity," 83.
21. Better Shelter, "Home Away from Home."
22. Williams, *Sustainable Design*, xxvii.
23. "Money and Art Happily Mated," 16.
24. Alfoldy, *Neocraft*, 21.
25. Harrod, *Real Thing*, 18
26. Kirkham, *Women Designers*, 98.
27. Buckley, in "Made in Patriarchy," notes that this is a general problem with objects made by women for their homes, which are expected to be used until they wear out or break and then be discarded.
28. "Louise Brigham, Crafts Expert."
29. "Money and Art Happily Mated," 16.
30. Thompson, "Louise Brigham."
31. Pigza, "Rescuing Cast Offs"; Weinberg, "Thinking Outside the Box."
32. Brigham makes several passing mentions of the idea that her designs can also be used "with artistic effect in the homes of wealth or culture," but this seems to be something of an afterthought.
33. "Exhibition to Aid Home Industries," 10.
34. Brigham did talk of teaching her HTA apprentices more advanced trade skills, but as far as I can tell, this never came to pass.

35. Crook, in "Craft and the Dialogics of Modernity" (17), posited the Arts and Crafts movement as a kind of alternative modernity.
36. Buckley, "Made in Patriarchy," 10.
37. Kirkham, *Women Designers*, 98.

Appendix: Timeline

Year: Event

September 2, 1840: Birth of LB's father, William Cleveland Brigham.

October 24, 1845: Birth of LB's mother, Maria Wilson Sheppard.

November 15, 1851: Birth of LB's future husband Henry Arnott Chisholm in Montreal, Canada.

January 10, 1875: Birth of Louise Ashton Brigham in Boston, MA, to William Cleveland Brigham and Maria Wilson Sheppard Brigham. LB's siblings are:

- Waldo Brigham (b. June 16, 1869–d. after June 5, 1880. Pope et al., in *Merriam Genealogy* [108], give an impossible date of 1863 for Waldo's death since he was listed as "at school" during the 1880 census).
- Lucy Merriam Brigham (April 23, 1873–date of death unknown but she survived her sister Anna Esther).
- Emma Sheppard Brigham (January 27–October 22, 1871).
- Anna Esther Brigham (February 9, 1876–March 10, 1945), m. Edward Metcalf Fisher.

May 19, 1877: Death of LB's mother.

December 27, 1877: Marriage of Henry Arnott Chisholm to his first wife, Eliza Gertrude Tozier (d. February 17, 1915), in Boston, MA. They have one child, André Tozier Chisholm (1879–1954).

December 4, 1894: Death of LB's father.

Ca. 1895–1897: LB studies art and education in New York City at the Pratt Institute, the Chase Art School, and the New York School of Art.

May 1897–October 1898: LB lives and teaches at the Pratt Institute's Neighborship Settlement, located in the Astral Apartments in Greenpoint, Brooklyn, NY.

Ca. 1900–1904: LB establishes and works at Sunshine Cottages, a settlement house, in Cleveland, OH.

1906: LB spends the summer on the island of Spitsbergen in the Svalbard Archipelago, where she experiments with making furniture from packing crates.

Fall 1905–ca. 1909: LB travels around Europe, studying arts and crafts in Sweden, Denmark, Holland, Scotland, Austria, and other countries.

1907: LB's second summer on Spitsbergen.

1909: LB publishes *Box Furniture*. That same year she furnishes her apartment at 539 E. 89th St., New York City, with box furniture and names it Box Corner First.

1910: LB organizes the inaugural exhibit of the Home Industries' Association (HIA) on E. 34th St. in New York City.

February 1911: LB shows a suite of box furniture at a Child Welfare Exhibit in New York City. The exhibit later travels around the country until 1913.

Winter 1911–1912: LB founds the Home Thrift Association, a woodworking center in Gracie Mansion in New York City. The HTA quickly outgrows the space and moves to 516 E. 89th St.

February–March 1913: The Women's Industrial Exposition at the Grand Central Palace in New York City includes an exhibit of LB's box furniture.

Ca. 1914: LB publishes *Illustrated Lectures* pamphlet.

1915: Second edition of *Box Furniture*.

1915: LB wins a medal at the Panama-Pacific International Exposition in San Francisco for her box furnishings for a Montessori School. She also exhibited box furniture in seven rooms of the Palace of Education at the exposition.

August 21, 1916: LB marries Henry Arnott Chisholm at the Mission Inn in Riverside, CA. They lived afterwards at 9107 Euclid Ave. in Cleveland.

Ca. 1915: LB founds Home Art Masters, a mail-order business for ready-to-assemble furniture, and starts up a furniture factory on New York City's Lower East Side.

Ca. 1918: LB opens a school and associated store at 16 Horatio St. in New York City to train young women in carpentry.

1919. Third edition of *Box Furniture*.

September 26, 1920. Death of Henry Arnott Chisholm in Yokohama, Japan.

1926. LB is living at Beechwood in Waterford, CT.

1927. LB is living at 111 Newbury Street, Boston, MA.

1936: LB has her first reading from Edgar Cayce.

Ca. 1936-1940: LB lives on and off with the Cayces.

1937: The Home Thrift Association moves to 350 E. 88th St. in New York City.

1940: The Home Thrift Association awards Brigham a medal in honor of a quarter century of service.

1945: LB spends some time at Unity Farm outside Kansas City, MO.

Mid-1950s: LB resides at the Sylvan Nursing Home in Trenton, NJ.

March 30, 1956: Death of LB at the Sylvan Nursing Home, aged 81.

Bibliography

Adamson, Glenn. *Thinking Through Craft*. Oxford: Berg, 2007.
Adkisson, Kevin. "Box Furniture: Thinking Outside the Box." Online publication (PDF), December 3, 2014, https://cpb-us-w2.wpmucdn.com/sites.udel.edu/dist/2/2059/files/2015/06/Adkisson_BoxFurnitureFinalDraftImages-18hsx0g.pdf.
Alfoldy, Sandra. *Neocraft: Modernity and the Crafts*. Halifax: The Press of the Nova Scotia College of Art and Design, 2007.
Aschermann, E. H., and G. G. Aschermann. "'Modern' Interior Decoration in American Homes." *International Studio* 53, no. 212 (October 1914): 81.
Attfield, Judith. "What Does History Have to Do with It? Feminism and Design History." *Journal of Design History* 16, no. 1 (2003): 78. (Review)
Aynsley, Jeremy. *Design and the Modern Magazine*. Manchester: Manchester University Press, 2007.
Aynsley, Jeremy, and Francesca Berry. "Publishing the Modern Home: Magazines and the Domestic Interior 1870–1965." *Journal of Design History* 18, no. 1 (2005): 1–5.
Bennett, C. *History of Manual and Industrial Education 1870–1917*. Peoria, IL: Chas. A. Bennett Co., 1937.
Berry, Martha. "Martha Berry to Louise Brigham Chisholm, April 7, 1928." In Martha Berry Digital Archive, https://mbda.berry.edu/items/show/6921.
Better Shelter. "A Home Away from Home," accessed August 20, 2019, http://bettershelter.org/about/.
"The Black and White Vogue." *The Upholsterer* 51, no. 6 (June 15, 1914).
"A Book of Boxes." *New York Times*, June 5, 1909.
"The Book of Knowledge." *Pittsburgh Press*, July 9, 1928.

"Book Notes." *The Federation Bulletin: A Magazine for the Woman of To-Day* 7, no. 1 (October 1909): 11.

"*Box Furniture*: by Louise Brigham." Book Reviews, *American Motherhood* 30, no. 5 (May 1910): 351.

"Box Furniture Development." *Furniture Manufacturer and Artisan*, May 1, 1916: 206.

"Boys Taught to Make Furniture Out of Boxes." *Christian Science Monitor*, January 25, 1913: 21.

Brigham, Louise. *Box Furniture: How to Make a Hundred Useful Articles for the Home*. Illustrations by Edward H. Aschermann from designs by the author. New York: Century Co., 1909.

———. *Box Furniture: How to Make a Hundred Useful Articles for the Home*. Illustrations by Edward H. Aschermann from designs by the author. New York: Century Co., 1915. 2nd ed.

———. *Box Furniture: How to Make a Hundred Useful Articles for the Home*. Illustrations by Edward H. Ascherman from designs by the author. New York: Century Co., 1919. 3rd ed. A copy of this edition with annotations by Louise Brigham is held in the Winterthur Museum, Garden, & Library.

———. "Dainty Curtains for a Girl's Room." *Ladies' Home Journal* 26 (May 1909): 47.

———. "A Dozen Good Work Aprons." *Ladies' Home Journal* 28, no. 2 (January 15, 1911): 12.

———. "How Boys Made Toys from Boxes." *St. Nicholas* 42, no. 5 (March 1915): 440–444.

———. "How Boys Make Furniture from Boxes." *St. Nicholas* 42. Published in 2 parts. Part I: no. 3 (January 1915): 241–244. Part II: no. 4 (February 1915): 339–343.

———. "How I Furnished My Entire Flat from Boxes." *Ladies' Home Journal* 27. Published in 4 parts. Part I: September 1, 1910: 70, 74. Part II (My Bedroom): October 1, 1910: 86, 92. Part III (My Dining Room): November 1, 1910: 80, 86. Part IV (My Kitchen): December 1, 1910: 68, 74.

———. "If a Girl Wants a New Curtain in Her Room." *Ladies' Home Journal* 28 (May 1, 1911): 75.

———. *Illustrated Lectures by Louise Brigham*. Publisher unknown, ca. 1914. (Pamphlet)

———. "Made for the Child from Boxes." *Ladies' Home Journal* 33 (May 1916): 43.

———. "Menu-Cards for Spring Luncheons." *Ladies' Home Journal* 26 (May 1909): 35.

———. "My Small City Apartment: How I Arranged to Get Much into Little Room." *Ladies' Home Journal* 26 (March 1909): 43.

———. "The New German Appliqué Work." *Ladies' Home Journal* 26 (March 1909): 39. (Byline: 'Selected by Louise Brigham')
———. "Rugs and Baskets Which Cost Nothing." *Ladies' Home Journal* 27 (August 1910): 31.
———. "Summer Novelties in Linen Appliqué." *Ladies' Home Journal* 26 (August 1909): 43.
———. "What Can Be Done with One Table." *Ladies' Home Journal* 27 (March 1910): 39.
———. "What I Did With My Spare Closet." *Ladies' Home Journal* 32 (January 1915): 47.
———. "What I Made from Ordinary Boxes." *Ladies' Home Journal* 26 (April 1909): 43.
Browett, Darren. "Reclaiming Simplicity, Thrift, and Utility." *Fortuitous Novelties* blog, October 16, 2012, http://fortuitousnovelties.wordpress.com/tag/louise-brigham/.
Buckley, Cheryl. "Made in Patriarchy: Toward a Feminist Analysis of Women and Design." *Design Issues* 3, no. 2 (Autumn 1986): 3–14.
Carter, Nanette. "Blueprint to Patterncraft: DIY Furniture Patterns and Packs in Postwar Australia." Design History Foundation, n.d., http://www.historiadeldisseny.org/congres/pdf/7%20Carter,%20Nanette%20%20BLUEPRINT%20TO%20PATTERNCRAFT%20DIY%20FURNITURE%20PATTERNS%20AND%20PACKS%20IN%20POST-WAR%20AUSTRALIA.pdf.
Clarage, Eleanor. "Main Street Meditations." *Plain Dealer* (Cleveland), February 4, 1929.
Clover, Faith M., and Kelly Hrenko. "Crafting Bridges Between Cultures in Minnesota: Birch Bark in Ojibwe and Scandinavian Crafts." In *Proceedings of the Crafticulation & Education Conference*, edited by Leena K. Kaukinen, 253–258. Helsinki: NordFo, 2009.
Combs, Heath E. "Sauder to Offer Replica of First RTA Table." *Furniture Today*, December 17, 2009.
"Contemporary American Bronzes." *The Bulletin of the Cleveland Museum of Art* 6, no. 10 (December 1919).
Crocker, John. "A Visit to 'Box Corner'." *National Magazine* 37 (October 1912–March 1913): 775–779.
Crook, Tom. "Craft and the Dialogics of Modernity: The Arts and Crafts Movement in Late Victorian and Edwardian England." *Journal of Modern Craft* 2, no. 1 (2009): 17–32.
Cuffley, Peter. *Australian Houses of the Forties and Fifties*. Knoxfield, VIC: Five Mile Press, 2007.
Denker, Bert, ed. *The Substance of Style: Perspectives on the American Arts and Crafts Movement*. Winterthur, DE: Henry Francis du Pont Winterthur Museum, 1996.

Dille, Marie. "Miss Louise Brigham, the Box-Woman." For "Women Who Lead the Way" column, *Dubuque Telegraph Herald*, November 12, 1915: 6.
Dole, Nathan Haskell, *America in Spitsbergen: The Romance of an Arctic Coal Mine*. Boston: Marshall Jones Company, 1922.
"Educational" column, *Association Men* 44 (September 1918): 315.
Edwards, Clive. "Furnishing a Home at the Turn of the Century: The Use of Furnishing Estimates from 1875 to 1910." *Journal of Design History* 4, no. 4 (1991): 233–239.
———. "'Home Is Where the Art Is': Women, Handicrafts and Home Improvements 1750–1900." *Journal of Design History* 19, no. 1 (2006): 11–21.
———. "Multum in Parvo: 'A Place for Everything and Everything in Its Place': Modernism, Space-Saving Bedroom Furniture and the Compactom Wardrobe." *Journal of Design History* 27, no. 1 (2013): 17–37.
"Eight Well-Furnished Rooms." Photographs by Arthur E. Marr and Henry Fuermann & Son. *Ladies' Home Journal* 27 (November 1, 1910): 81.
"Exhibition to Aid Home Industries." *New York Times*, November 20, 1910: 10.
Eyestone, J. "The Influence of Swedish Sloyd and Its Interpreters on American Art Education." *Studies in Art Education* 34, no. 1 (1992): 28–38.
Ferry, Emma. "'Any Lady Can Do This Without Much Trouble …': Class and Gender in The Dining Room (1878)." *Interiors* 5, no. 2 (2014).
———. "Introduction" (to Part I). In *Designing the Modern Interior: From the Victorians to Today*, edited by Penny Sparke, Anne Massey, Trevor Keeble, and Brenda Martin, 13–30. New York: Berg, 2000.
Fitzgerald, Oscar P. *American Furniture: 1650 to the Present*. Lanham, MD: Rowman & Littlefield, 2018.
Forster, Matt. *Backroads & Byways of Ohio: Drives, Day Trips & Weekend Excursions*. New York: Countryman Press, 2018.
Frederick, Christine. *The New Housekeeping: Efficiency Studies in Home Management*. New York: Doubleday, Page & Co., 1913.
"Furniture Advertising in America." *The Upholsterer* 51, no. 6 (June 15, 1914).
"Furniture from Boxes." *San Jose Evening News*, June 30, 1909: 2.
Gelber, Steven M. *Hobbies: Leisure and the Culture of Work in America*. New York: Columbia University Press, 1999.
Giedion, Siegfried. *Mechanization Takes Command*. New York: Norton, 1969.
Gillespie, Harriet. "Women Who Count." *San Francisco Call* 111, no. 94 (March 3, 1912): 9.
"The Glass Classroom." American Montessori Society website, accessed January 12, 2014, http://amshq.org/Montessori-Education/History-of-Montessori-Education/the_glass_classroom.aspx.
Goffman, Erving. *The Presentation of Self in Everyday Life*. London: Harmondsworth, 1978.

Grier, Katherine C. *Culture and Comfort: People, Parlors, and Upholstery 1850–1930.* Rochester, NY: Strong Museum, 1988.
Griswold, Bernice. "What Women Are Doing to Help Win the War: Girl Artists Take Up Saw and Hammer in Interest of Brand New War Art." *Plain Dealer* (Cleveland), September 29, 1918.
"A Guide to the New Books." *The Literary Digest*, August 7, 1909: 207.
Hagel, Caia. "Democratic Design: The Work of Le Van Bo." *Dwell*, August 17, 2012, https://www.dwell.com/article/democratic-design-the-work-of-le-van-bo-20205cf2.
Hall, A. Neely. *The Boy Craftsman: Practical and Profitable Ideas for a Boy's Leisure Hours.* Boston: Lothrop, Lee & Shephard, 1905.
———. *Handicrafts for Handy Boys: Practical Plans for Work and Play with Many Ideas for Earning Money.* London: T. Werner Laurie, 1912.
———. "A Small Toboggan Slide That Any Boy Can Build." *St. Nicholas* 42 (January 1915): 245–247.
Harrod, Tanya. *The Real Thing: Essays on Making in the Modern World.* London: Hyphen Press, 2015.
Hartnell, Cameron C. "Arctic Network Builders: The Arctic Coal Company's Operations on Spitsbergen and Its Relationship with the Environment." PhD diss., Michigan Technological University, 2009.
Hauser, Mary E. *Learning from Children: The Life and Legacy of Caroline Pratt.* New York: Peter Lang, 2006.
Helland, Janice. "'Good Work and Clever Design': Early Exhibitions of the Home Arts and Industries Association." *Journal of Modern Craft* 5, no. 3: 275–293.
Hewitt, Emma Churchman. *Queen of the Home: Her Reign from Infancy to Age, from Attic to Cellar.* Philadelphia: W.W. Houston, 1889.
Hill, Rosemary. *God's Architect: Pugin and the Building of Romantic Britain.* New Haven: Yale University Press, 2007.
Hiller, N. R. *The Hoosier Cabinet in Kitchen History.* Bloomington: Indiana University Press, 2009.
Holloway, Edward Stratton. *The Practical Book of Furnishing the Small House and Apartment.* Philadelphia: J. B. Lippincott, 1922.
"Home Art Masters advertisement." *The Masses* 6, no. 10 (July 1915): 27.
Houze, Rebecca. "From *Wiener Kunst im Hause* to the Wiener Werkstätte: Marketing Domesticity with Fashionable Interior Design." *Design Issues* 18, no. 1 (Winter 2000): 3–23.
Howes, Durward, ed. "Chisholm, Louise Brigham." In *American Women: The Official Who's Who Among Women III: 1939–40*, 164. Los Angeles: Richard Blank Publishing, 1935.
Ingham, John N. *Biographical Dictionary of American Business Leaders.* Santa Barbara, CA: Greenwood Publishing Group, 1983.

Jencks, Charles, and Nathan Silver. *Adhocism*. Cambridge, MA: MIT Press, 2013. (Originally published 1972.)

Kallman, Theodore P. "Pilgrimage of Ralph Albertson (1866–1951): Modern American Liberalism and the Pursuit of Happiness." PhD diss., Georgia State University, 1997.

Kardon, Janet, ed. *The Ideal Home 1900–1920: The History of Twentieth Century American Craft*. New York: Harry N. Abrams/American Craft Museum, 1993.

Kirkham, Pat. *Women Designers in the USA, 1900–2000: Diversity and Difference*. New Haven: Yale University Press, 2000.

Kirkpatrick, Sidney. *Edgar Cayce: An American Prophet*. New York: Riverhead Books, 2001.

Kirkpatrick, Sidney, and Nancy Kirkpatrick. "Louise Brigham: The Inn-Keeper's Daughter." Unpublished manuscript.

Klein, Alexander. "Personal Income of U.S. States: Estimates for the Period 1880–1910." In *Warwick Economic Research Papers*, no. 916, Department of Economics, University of Warwick. See visualization at http://web.stanford.edu/group/spatialhistory/cgi-bin/railroaded/gallery/interactive-visualizations/capita-income-united-states-1880-1910.

Lacroix, Mary. *The Remnant*. New York: Avon Books, 1981. Reissued by A.R.E. Press, 1989.

Laitio, Tommi. "From Best Design to Just Design." In *Open Design Now: Why Design Cannot Remain Exclusive*, edited by Bas van Abel, Lucas Evers, Roel Klaassen, and Peter Troxler, 190–201. Amsterdam, The Netherlands: BIS Publishers, 2011.

Landis, Scott. *Conservation by Design*. Museum of Art, Rhode Island School of Design, and Woodworkers Alliance for Rainforest Protection, 1993.

Larrabee, Eric, and Rolf Meyersohn, eds. *Mass Leisure*. Glencoe, IL: The Free Press, 1958.

Larsson, Gustav. *Sloyd*. Boston: Sloyd Training School, 1902.

Leavitt, Sarah A. *From Catharine Beecher to Martha Stewart: A Cultural History of Domestic Advice*. Chapel Hill: University of North Carolina Press, 2002.

Lees-Maffei, Grace. "Introduction: Professionalization as a Focus in Interior Design History." *Journal of Design History* 21, no. 1 (2008): 1–18. (Special issue: Professionalizing Interior Design 1870–1970.)

"Library of Congress Copyright Office." *Catalogue of Copyright Entries: Part 1, Group 2*. New Series, vol. 12, no. 9. Washington, DC: Government Printing Office, 1915.

"Louise Chisholm, Crafts Expert, 81." *New York Times*, March 31, 1956: 15.

MacDonald, Juliette. "The Value of 'Sloppy Craft': Creativity and Community." In *Sloppy Craft: Postdisciplinarity and the Crafts*, edited by Elaine Cheasley Paterson and Susan Surette, 93–108. London: Bloomsbury Publishing, 2015.

"Making Box Furniture: Its Practical and Ethical Value." *The Craftsman* 21, no. 2 (November 1911): 218–221.

Mancini, J. M. *Pre-modernism: Art World Change and American Culture from the Civil War to the Armory Show*. Princeton, NJ: Princeton University Press, 2005.

Mari, Enzo. *Autoprogettazione*. Mantua, Italy: Edizioni Corraini, 1974.

McClain, Aurora, and Christopher Long. "Aschermanns." *Antiques*, January–February 2011, http://www.themagazineantiques.com/articles/aschermanns/.

McDonough, William, and Michael Braungart. *Cradle to Cradle*. New York: North Point Press, 2002.

McLaren, Christine. "Hartz IV Möbel: 'It's Not About Furniture. It's About the Quality of Life'." Guggenheim Museum, June 2, 2012, https://www.guggenheim.org/blogs/lablog/hartz-iv-mobel-its-not-about-furniture-its-about-the-quality-of-life.

Meikle, Jeffrey L. *Design in the USA*. Oxford History of Art. Oxford: Oxford University Press, 2005.

"Miracles with Old Boxes: Wonderful Furniture in an East Side Flat." *The Sun*, August 28, 1909: 3.

"Miss Brigham Makes Furniture from Boxes." *Lexington Herald*, September 22, 1909.

"Money and Art Happily Mated." *Los Angeles Times*, August 22, 1916: 16.

Morris, William. "The Beauty of Life." In *Prose, Lectures, and Essays*, edited by G. D. H. Cole. London: Nonesuch Library, 1934.

Nasser, Farah. "Multifunctional Furniture for Underprivileged Communities: A Milestone in Sustainable Development." MS thesis, Purdue University, Department of Computer Graphics Technology, 2013, http://docs.lib.purdue.edu/cgttheses/26.

"Needy Thousands Get Bounty Here." *New York Times*, November 25, 1938.

"News from the Classes." *Harvard Graduates' Magazine* 29, no. 113 (September 1920): 276.

"New York Book Announcements." *New York Times*, April 24, 1909.

"Notes of the Week: Monthly Charity Conference." *Charities: A Weekly Journal of Philanthropy and Social Advance* 14 (April 29, 1905): 692.

"Old Wooden Boxes Turned into Pretty Furniture, Novel and Practical Idea of Miss Louise Brigham." *Christian Science Monitor*, July 23, 1909: 6.

Ovington, Mary White. "Annual Report of the Neighborship Settlement." *Pratt Institute Monthly* 7, no. 1 (November 1898): 6–14.

Parker, Roszika. *The Subversive Stitch: Embroidery and the Making of the Feminine*. London: I.B. Tauris, 2010.

Paterson, Elaine Cheasley, and Susan Surette, eds. *Sloppy Craft: Postdisciplinarity and the Crafts*. London: Bloomsbury Publishing, 2015.

"Pen and Brush Club Opens Bazaar Dec. 10." *New York Times*, November 18, 1936.

"Pen and Brush Club Opens Its Sale Today." *New York Times*, December 10, 1936.

"Pen Women to Give Luncheon." *New York Times*, October 18, 1936.

Pigza, Jessica M. "Rescuing Cast Offs: The Do-It-Yourself Box Furniture of Social Worker Louise Brigham." *The Readex Report*, September 2009, http://www.newsbank.com/readex/newsletters.cfm?newsletter=22&article=34.

"Planning the Women's Industrial Exposition." *New York Times*, February 9, 1913: 2.

Pope, Charles Henry, Charles Pierce Merriam, C. E. Gildersome-Dickinson, and James Sheldom Merriam. *Merriam Genealogy in England and America*. Boston: Charles H. Pope, 1906: 108.

Priestman, Mabel Tuke. *Art and Economy in Home Decoration*. New York: John Lane Company, 1908.

Priestman, Mabel Tuke. *Handicrafts in the Home*. Chicago: A. C. McClurg, 1910.

Provenzo, Eugene F., and Arlene Brett. *The Complete Block Book*. New York: Syracuse University Press, 1982.

"Puppet Show Helps Home Thrift Clubs." *New York Times*, November 20, 1939.

Reif, Rita. "The Subtle Artistry of the Furniture of Harvey Ellis." *New York Times*, April 12, 1981.

"Reviews." *The Craftsman* 16, no. 5 (August 1909). (Review of *Box Furniture*)

Rich, Ednah Anne. *Paper Sloyd: A Handbook for Primary Grades*. Boston: Ginn & Co., 1905.

Richardson, Lucy Ryder. *102 Midcentury Chairs and Their Stories*. London: Pavilion Books, 2016.

Rothschild, Joan, ed. *Design and Feminism: Re-visioning Spaces, Places, and Everyday Things*. New Brunswick, NJ: Rutgers University Press, 1999.

"Rostand Praised Catulle Mendes." *New York Times*, April 3, 1909.

Russell, Frank. *A Century of Chair Design*. New York: Rizzoli, 1985.

Scharnhorst, Gary. *Bret Harte: Opening the American Literary West*. Norman: University of Oklahoma Press, 2000.

Shields, David S. "Studio, Moffett." Broadway Photographs website, accessed April 14, 2015, http://broadway.cas.sc.edu/content/studio-moffett.

Showalter, J. C., and J. T. Driesbach, *Wooton Patent Desks: A Place for Everything and Everything in Its Place*. Oakland: Indiana State Museum, 1983.

"Six Women Honored for Welfare Work; Gold Medals Given to Directors of Home Thrift Association." *New York Times*, November 20, 1940: 8.

Smith, Bertha H. "The Gospel of Simplicity as Applied to Tenement Homes." *The Craftsman* 9, no. 1 (October 1905): 83–90.

Sparke, Penny, Anne Massey, Trevor Keeble, and Brenda Martin, eds. *Designing the Modern Interior: From the Victorians to Today*. New York: Berg, 2000.

Stowe, Doug. "Tools, Hands, and the Expansion of Intellect." In *Proceedings of the Crafticulation & Education Conference*, edited by Leena K. Kaukinen. Helsinki: Nordic Forum for Research and Development in Craft and Design, 2009.

Strasser, Susan. *Waste and Want: A Social History of Trash*. New York: Henry Holt, 1999.

"Teaching Boys to Make Good Furniture Out of Boxes." *New York Times*, January 19, 1913: 10.

Thompson, Neville. "Louise Brigham: Developer of Box Furniture." In *The Substance of Style: Perspectives on the American Arts and Crafts Movement*, edited by Bert Denker. Winterthur, DE: Henry Francis du Pont Winterthur Museum, 1996.

Thorell, Marge. *Karin Bergöö Larsson and the Emergence of Swedish Design*. Jefferson, NC: McFarland & Company, 2019.

"Three-Day Bazaar Will Be Held Next Month by Pen and Brush Club to Aid Its Charities." *New York Times*, November 29, 1936.

Van Abel, Bas, Lucas Evers, Roel Klaassen, and Peter Troxler, eds. *Open Design Now: Why Design Cannot Remain Exclusive*. Amsterdam, The Netherlands: BIS Publishers, 2011.

Weinberg, Larry. "Thinking Outside the Box: Louise Brigham's Furniture of 1909." December 10, 2009, http://www.interiordesign.net/blog/Cindy_s_Salon/35211-Thinking_Outside_the_Box_Louise_Brigham_s_Furniture_of_1909.php.

Wellhousen, Karyn, and Judith E. Kieff. *A Constructivist Approach to Block Play in Early Childhood*. Albany, NY: Delmar, 2001.

"What They Read." *Vogue* 34, no. 1 (July 1909): 21.

Williams, Daniel E. *Sustainable Design: Ecology, Architecture, and Planning*. Hobocken, NJ: Wiley, 2007.

Windsor, Henry Haven. "Mission Furniture: How to Make It." *Popular Mechanics*, 1909.

"Women's Work, Women's Clubs." *Los Angeles Times*, May 28, 1915, II–6.

Zeisel, Joseph S. "The Workweek in American Industry 1850–1956." In *Mass Leisure*, edited by Eric Larrabee and Rolf Meyersohn, 145–153. Glencoe, IL: The Free Press, 1958.

Index

A
Advent Bay, 4
advice writing, 32, 33, 61
Albers, Anni, 100
Ammons, Theodosia, 62
Amundsen, Roald, 2
Andrée, Salomon, 2
Arctic Coal Company, 4
Art at Home (books), 32
Art Nouveau, 3, *23*, 100
Arts and Crafts movement, 3, 38, 100, 106
Aschermann, Edward H., 21, 40, 56, 100, 110
   color palette, 42
   drawings, 41–42
Aschermann, Gladys, 40
Asherman, Edward H. *See* Aschermann, Edward H.
Astral Apartments, 20

B
basketry, 5, 17, 44, 62
Bauhaus, 37
Beecher, Catherine, 32
Berry, Martha, 89
Box Corner First, 52, 56, 59, 71
Box Corner Second, 56
Box Corner Third, 56
box furniture, 50, 71, 74, 89, 99, 108
   camping, 71
   cost of, 21, 32, 58, 61
   factory, 78, 89
   school, 78
   survival of, 31, 108
   toys, 69, 78
   workshops, 59, 68, 70, 74
Box Furniture (1909), 2, 77, 94
   Club-room Corner Seat, 21
   College Corner Seat, 37
   color palette, 42
   Combination Reading Desk, 26, 30
   Copenhagen Sideboard, 21
   Double Wall Rack, 37
   drawings for, 41–42
   Dressing Table, 102

Flower and Book Stand, 37
Flower Stand, 102
Game-table, 21
Greek-cross Tea-table, 51, 54
Invalid's Bed Table, 79
Large Wall Book Rack, 37
organization of, 30
plagiarism of, 77
Plant-box, 26
price of, 32
publication of, 26
Small Wall Rack, 37
Spitzbergen Sideboard, 30
translations of, 77
Window-seat, 37
Box Furniture (1919), 85
Octagon Nursery Table, 87
Box Nest, *64*
Braungart, Michael, 105
Brigham, Anna Esther, 13
Brigham, Louise
apartments, 35, 51, 52, 56, 62, 69, 89
in Copenhagen, 17, 21
death, 97
and Edgar Cayce, 92, 96
education, 15, 20
European travels, 16, 73
family, 13
finances, 14, 95
health, 21, 95–97
lost memoir, 93, 96
marriage, 88
monogram, 19
psychic readings, 93–96
and reincarnation, 93, 94
social worker, 20
on Spitsbergen, 2, 4–6
and Unity Church, 96
Brigham, Lucy Merriam, 13
Brigham, Maria Wilson Sheppard, 13
Brigham, Waldo, 13

Brigham, William Cleveland, 13
Bruere, Martha Bensley, 22

C
Carpenter Gothic, 40
carpentry. *See* woodworking
Cayce, Edgar, 90, 91
chairs, 21, 58, 71
Adirondack chair, 39
Crate Chair, 3, 101, 102
Morris chair, 56, 69
Chase School of Art, 15, 20
Child, Lydia Maria, 32
Child Welfare Exhibit, 58, 68
Chisholm, Andre Tozier, 88
Chisholm, Eliza Gertrude, 88
Chisholm, Henry Arnott, 88–89, 94
Chisholm, Louise Brigham. *See* Brigham, Louise
Chisholm, Mrs. Henry. *See* Brigham, Louise
Chisholm Steel Shovel Works, 88
Church, Frederic, 2
Cintrangulo, Augusto, 103
Clemens, James B., 68
Cleveland Institute of Art. *See* Western Reserve School of Design
Cleveland Rolling Mill, 88
coal mining, 3
color
and Edward H. Aschermann, 42
and Louise Brigham, 21, 42, 53, 56, 87
Cooper Union. *See* New York School for Design
The Craftsman, 35, 40, 77
curtains, 21

D
Danes Island, 2, 8
Davis, Gladys, 93, 94, 96, 97

Davis, Katharine Bement, 61
design
   do-it-yourself, 3, 26, 69, 74, 102, 109
   education, 103
   and gender, 9, 15, 16, 44, 68, 78
   maker spaces, 74, 103
   modern, 10, 42, 43, 87, 100, 107
   modular, 3, 26, 35–37, 103
   multifunctional, 3, 26, 35, 103, 105
   open source, 3, 103
   recycled materials, 3, 21, 31, 33, 34, 102, 103, 109
   sustainable, 3, 34, 102
Deskey, Donald, 37
desks, 6, 26, 30, 35, 36, 52, 55, 58, *64*
De Stijl, 3, 31, 100, 101
Dewey, John, 72

E
Edwards, Clive, 10
Ellis, Harvey, 40
embroidery, 16
Erikson, Lars, 73

F
fancy work, 15
Flanagan, Edward J., 71
folk art, 20, 54, 89
Frederick, Christine, 43
French, Daniel Chester, 89
Froebel toys, 20
furniture, 35–37
   from barrels, 31
   camping, 71, 81, 82, 88
   children's, 31, 51, 58
   ready-to-assemble, 3, 79, 81, 88
   rustic, 39
   space-saving, 35

G
Gilbreth, Frank Sr., 43
Globe Wernicke, 37
Goffman, Erving, 51
Goncharova, Natalia, 55
Gracie Mansion, 68, 71, 72, 106
Gwenthean Cottage, 62

H
Hale, Sarah Josepha, 32
Hall, A. Neely, 77
Hammerfest, 4
Harte, Ethel Bret, *64n27*
Hartz IV Möbel, 103
Henry Street settlement, 61
Hesse, Eva, 102
Hoffmann, Josef, 17, 26, 39, 40, 56, 100, 110
Home Art Masters, 79, 82, 88, 89
Home Arts and Industries Association, 60, 74
Home Industries' Association (HIA), 60, 114
Home Thrift Association (HTA), 62, 68, 70, 74, 79
Hunter, Dard, 40
Hunter, William Joseph. *See* Hunter, Dard

I
Ice Fjord, 4, 5
IKEA, 37, 52, 79, 81, 88, 103, 106, 107
Illustrated Lectures, 56
I-Ma-Da Furniture, 79
interior design, 16, 32, 45

J
Jugendstil, 3

K

Kahn, Michael, 102
Karasz, Ilonka, 54, 101
Kittredge, Mabel Hyde, 44, 61

L

Lacroix, Mary, 94
Ladies' Home Journal, 43, 44, 50, 52, 68
Lane, Cynthia P., 29
Larsson, Carl, 17
Larsson, Gustav, 73
Larsson, Karin, 17
Lee, Thomas, 39
Le-Mentzel, Van Bo, 103
Levy, Arthur S., 79
Livant, Leda, 102
Longyearbyen. *See* Longyear City
Longyear City, 4–6, 8
Longyear, John Munro, 3, 4

M

Macintosh, Charles Rennie, 17, 20, 57
Mackail, H.W., 9
Malevich, Kasimir, 55
Mari, Enzo, 102
McDonough, William, 105
metal work, 17
Mission style, 39, 40, 100
model home, 44, 61–62, 105
modern art, 16, 55
Montessori School, 59, 115
Morris, William, 7, 9, 38, 107, 110
Munroe, William Dearborn, 4

N

Nasser, Farah, 104
National League of American Pen Women, 95
needlework, 5

nested benches, 21, 36
Newman, George A., 52
New York Charity Organization Society, 21
New York School for Design, 15
New York School of Art. *See* Chase School of Art
New York Society for Decorative Art, 16
Nobile, Umberto, 2

P

packing crates, 26, 31, 34, 37, 40, 55, 68, 70, 78, 101
  as fuel, 29
  standardization of, 29
Panama-Pacific International Exposition, 49, 59, 115
Parsons The New School for Design. *See* Chase School of Art
Philadelphia School of Design, 15
Pipestone Indian School, 71
Prairie School, 3, 39
Pratt Institute, 15, 20
Pratt Institute Neighborhood Association, 20
Progressive movement, 16, 33, 39
  and hygiene, 43
Pugin, Augustus, 81
Pullman, Philip, 4

R

Reiss, Winold, 100
The Remnant, 94
Rietveld, Gerrit, 3, 87, 101
Riis, Jacob, 29
Rohde, Gilbert, 37
Rookwood Pottery, 78
Roycroft Press, 40
Ruskin, John, 38

S

Salix polaris, 6
Salomon, Otto, 73
Sauder, Erie, 81
Schütte-Lihotzky, Margarete, 101
settlement movement, 20, 21, 39, 57, 61
   Cleveland, 20
   Copenhagen, 21
   Hull House, 22
   Sunshine Cottage, 88
sewing, 5
Shackleton, Ernest, 2
sideboards, 6, 21, 30
sloyd movement, 72–73
   Sloyd Institute, 17, 73
   Sloyd Teacher Training School, 73
Smith-Hughes Act, 79
Soleri, Paolo, 102
Spitsbergen, 1–5, 8, 17, 21, 71, 89
Spitzbergen. *See* Spitsbergen
St. Nicholas, 78
Stickley, Gustav, 35, 39, 40, 56, 69, 77, 87, 100, 110
Storer, Maria Longworth, 78
Sunshine Cottage, 20, 21, 88. *See also* settlement movement
Svalbard, 2–6, 71, 81
   Svalbard Treaty, 3
Sylvan Nursing Home, 97

T

tableware, 20
Tak-Apart Furniture, 71, 82, 88
Taylor, Frederick, 43
Tedrow, Altha, 71, 109
textiles, 20, 55
Thompson, Neville, 17, 109
Tinguely, Jean, 102
Toppelius, Meri, 73
trash, 34, 68
Tutankhamun, 89

U

Unity Church, 96
Unity Farm, 96
Unity Village. *See* Unity Farm

V

Vienna Secession, 3, 17, 40
vocational training, 70

W

wall treatments, 42, 54, 93
Ward, Frederick, 81
weaving, 17, 44, 55
Wellman, Walter, 2, 8
Western Reserve School of Design, 15
Wheeler, Candace, 16
Whitney, Gertrude Vanderbilt, 89
Wiener Werkstätte, 17, 19, 40, 100
William Chisholm's Sons Company, 88
Women's Industrial Exposition, 49, 59
woodworking, 17, 29, 31, 60, 71, 110
   finishes, 39, 40
   tools, 5, 7, 15, 26, 29, 68, 73, 85, 102
World's Columbian Exposition, 61
Wright, Frank Lloyd, 20, 39, 55, 57
Wright, Julia McNair, 32

Y

YMCA, 79